I0132535

God's Wake-Up Call

71 Short Stories
Each with a Moral

Parables for our Times
Modern Psalms

Nancy Goldberg Hilton

God's Wake-Up Call

71 Short Stories Each with a Moral

Parables for our Times
Modern Psalms
Written by Nancy Goldberg Hilton

Book editor - Della Hilton

God's Wake-Up Call
© copyright September, 2011 by Nancy Goldberg Hilton
All rights reserved

No part of this book may be reproduced in any form whatsoever, whether by graphic, visual, electronic, filming, microfilming, tape, recording or any other means, without the written permission of the author, except in the case of brief passages embodied in critical reviews and articles where the title, author, and ISBN accompany such a review or article. Limited, non-commercial, private use is allowed.

ISBN
0-9776403-8-8
978-0-9776403-8-6

Library of Congress number TX 7-474-166, November 28, 2011 by Nancy Mae Goldberg Hilton

Published by HiltonBooks LLC, September 2011

This book is dedicated to the Glory of God.

The image on the cover is a picture of the Mount Redoubt, Alaska eruption, taken April 21, 1990 by R. Clucas (110 miles SW of Anchorage, Alaska). Ascending eruption cloud from Redoubt Volcano as viewed to the west from the en: Kenai Peninsula. The image is in the public domain because it contains materials that originally came from the United States Geological Survey, an agency of the United States Department of Interior.

The cover was created by Candelaria Atalaya

TABLE OF CONTENTS

CHAPTER 4 | SOLUTIONS UNLOCKED

CHAPTER 5 | JOURNEYS

CHAPTER 6 | THE SYMPHONY OF LIFE

CHAPTER 7 | CHOICES

CHAPTER 8 | THOUGHTS

CHAPTER 9 | THE END TIMES

CHAPTER 10 | YOUR STORY

GOD'S WAKE-UP CALL

> I pour my heart out to God.
> I sing praises to my Father in Heaven.
> I rejoice in the beauty of deliverance by my
> Savior and Messiah, Jesus Christ.
> I am no longer wandering in this world alone.
> I know the answers to my deepest questions.
> I have heard God's Wake-Up Call.

1 | THERE ARE STORIES INSIDE EACH OF US

There are stories inside each of us.
They are the stories of our own struggles and choices.
They are the stories of our human nature and growth.
They are the stories of our achievements, our trials, and failures.

But all of these stories have a very important connection and purpose. They are meant to increase our spiritual understanding of our value and potential as human beings. Each one of us is on a journey and is looking for answers.

Sometimes it is necessary to seek solutions that we cannot see.
Sometimes it is necessary to step out in faith and find the true purpose of our lives.

I did this through a conversion from Judaism to Christianity. I found the way to solve the loneliness and emptiness that was inside of me. But changing my religion was only the first step. I had much to learn about my own responsibility and our responsibilities to each other. We live in a world that is connected through communication and human and spiritual interaction. What we do today reaches into tomorrow and then into eternity.

I have written a series of spiritual short stories. Each story is meant to engender a thought process of evaluating our lives from a spiritual point of view.
I have learned that we are more than we can see.
We are more than whims of the winds that blow us from one side to another.
We have great spirits inside these minds and bodies. We must try to live beyond our sight and begin to understand that God, Jesus Christ and the Holy Ghost exist and have provided us with a plan of salvation.

The laws of God are in place. It is not a hard plan to understand. It is just hard to realize that there is a penalty beyond earthly justice if we do not improve our ways.

What is the truth of your spiritual life?
Only you can decide.

2 | BETWEEN TWO WORLDS – THE TEMPORAL AND THE SPIRITUAL

How do you define the space between two worlds? Is there a separation or can they co-exist in harmony? What worlds am I talking about?

We live in a world filled with all kinds of variety—in every location we find different habits, dress, and language, different experiences, talents and goals. We have been described as a melting pot of humanity all mixed together and then separated into classes and borders of our own making. What are our values? How do we view one another? Do we see our differences or our similarities? What would we change in this world? What behavior would we like from every human being on earth? Should there be more honesty, integrity, trustworthiness, chastity and morality? Should there be peace and harmony, safety and security?

Wouldn't it be wonderful if, in an instant, we could change and everyone could shed their outward appearance and we could see the true value of our spiritual natures? Would this be loving? Would we break apart the walls of misunderstanding and ignorance and seek the goodness in each person as well as in ourselves?

The world that we live in is fraught with challenges, questions, and choices. It is displayed in living color upon large screens that invade our minds and disturb our thoughts. It is both disabling and joyful. It is traumatic and invigorating. It is challenging and overwhelming.

How do we bridge the gaps in this world? Who are we? Why are we here? What is our purpose? Why even ask? Isn't it enough to just survive until the end?

3 | MY STORY

I have a story to tell you that is true. I have traveled miles in order to find the answers to these questions and in the end, the answer found me; but then began the quest for more knowledge. I hope that you will read on.

When I was a young Jewish girl, I always wondered who I would be when I grew up. Would I be a doctor, lawyer or Indian chief? I would peer into the sky and wish upon a star. I would ask, "What is eternity? Where does it begin and end?" I always wanted the answers to these questions. I could not understand how I fit into the total plan.

As a young Jewish girl, I sang the Hebrew songs to God. As I grew older, I continued to practice my religion, but did I believe it? I went to the synagogue twice a year, if that, and celebrated all the Jewish holidays with my family. It is not that I thought I had all my spiritual answers. I just didn't think I needed help from any religious source. The world tried to teach me that I should know it all with or without a belief in God.

When I graduated from college, I went to work to provide for my living expenses. I picked a field of work that I could excel in. This was it, I thought. I would be the very best in my chosen field. I would be the youngest and brightest. So I went at this work with a quest for knowledge and a goal to excel. Along the path, I worked harder and harder and longer and longer hours. I kept up this ugly pace for years and years. I was promoted and promoted again. I changed companies and grew in stature and attained my goal. According to worldly standards, I was doing well. My work consumed my life. I was my work!

I built walls of safety around myself to keep me from feeling very much and to stay focused only on my work, but eventually the walls started moving in. They kept on moving just a little closer each day until all I could see were the walls. Emptiness grew inside of me. I pictured myself with a large hole in the middle, like a cut-out paper doll with the insides missing. I was a shell dressed for business and working at a frantic pace. Why did I do all of this work? To make money? Of course! Money is necessary, but is it the total answer to everything? Shouldn't I be happy? Can't money buy anything in this world? I had a nice home and a car. I had things and more things. That was what money was for, wasn't it? I would buy things and they would make me happy, right? But the things owned me. I became their caretaker, their provider. I was working to support these things. But where was my happiness?

What were the answers to the riddle of my life? Why did I feel like a jigsaw puzzle whose pieces did not fit? It was as if a giant, dark hand had taken the most precious gifts of my life and kept them hidden from view. I could not see. I was blind.

I decided to investigate the psychic world because it was a popular subject. I was hoping to find some answers from a higher, spiritual source. In the psychic world, I heard terms like "spirit guide" or "higher self." I did not understand these terms, but everyone told me I would find my answers. Did I believe them? I was not sure, for their lives also contained a frantic search for their own meaning and I did not think that the answers they received from the psychic arena helped them very much. They often complained about their feelings of inadequacy and disappointment. But I just kept searching for answers so I could get spiritual, not just earthly help.

In spite of this new quest for spiritual understanding, the emptiness inside of me grew and thoughts of worthlessness and even suicide would flood my mind. I would hear, "Stop the pain. End this existence. Who would care? You have no value. You are nothing. Erase yourself from the face of this earth."

I would listen to this flow of words and wake up from my nightmares screaming out loud. I was walking in quicksand and not able to move away fast enough from the things that chased me in the night.

Now, you are probably thinking I was having an anxiety attack. I had no idea what was happening. I did not take drugs, smoke or drink alcohol. I just knew that because of my quest for spiritual understanding I had possibly opened a door that I now wanted to shut tight. The spirit world was real.

I knew I needed to get away from the everyday events of my life, so I decided to take a vacation. That should work. I would be free to choose my own way and make my own schedule outside of the borders of my routine life.

I boarded a plane to Arizona. This was a land of contrasts ranging from steep red rocks to pine trees, a beautiful place containing dizzying depths of the Grand Canyon to the dry, flat desert.

For a while I was free of all the cares that I had left behind. I drove along curving roads amidst beautiful canyons, but I had not escaped the voice of destruction in my head that got louder and louder. As I continued to travel the roads of life, the voice continued to enter my mind: "Listen to my words!" I could not escape from the emptiness inside of me. It was with me wherever I traveled and whatever I did.

During my visit to Arizona, I sought for a way to connect with my Spiritual Guide. I did not realize that there were evil spirits in addition to good ones and that the results of this quest might open spiritual doors that I could not close. I expected a peaceful journey surrounded by white light traveling through space and time. I did have a spiritual experience, but it was definitely not peaceful.

As I innocently asked for a spiritual guide to help me in life, the reality of a vast spirit world became apparent to me and I realized that I was ill-equipped to handle what was happening. What I felt was a huge evil force that was beyond my comprehension. I can tell you that evil beings are real. They are not cartoon characters or frightening creatures in movies. They are real and powerful, and I was afraid!

After this happened, I tried to rest. As soon as I closed my eyes I had what you could say were vivid nightmares. Sleep left me for fear that I would not awaken. I was sick to my stomach and could not eat. I was like an innocent child facing a mighty force that I did not understand. This was not a drug-, food-, or alcohol-related event as I never partook of those substances. It was real!

Thoughts of my death coursed through my mind as I continued through this strange world of darkness. I yearned for something or someone to help me, but who or what?

If I thought I had problems before, this new event just compounded them enormously. Obviously, I had not made a good choice.

Two days after my frightening experience I arrived in Page, Arizona for a two-and-one-half hour boat trip from Wahweap Marina to Rainbow Bridge. I felt nauseous and had eaten very little during those two days.

I had always wanted to see Rainbow Bridge. For some reason, I was very anxious to get there. I felt a great sense of urgency.

The trip was magnificent as the lake is filled with huge, red rocks jutting out of the water. The boat turned into a side channel and finally arrived at the dock leading to the Bridge. We were told there was a one-half mile hike to the Bridge and that we must return in 45 minutes. I was the first one off the boat and walked quickly across the long dock to the sandy path that led to the Bridge. The first sight of this magnificent, naturally-formed Bridge that spans this side canyon was thrilling. I was amazed at its height and beauty. But most of all, I was happy to feel a sense of peace that came upon me. I felt safe here.

I walked under the Bridge and up the small hill next to it. I found a place to sit and rest. I looked around and saw hundreds of people from the excursion boats milling around. I thought to myself, "It would be nice to be here alone." I was so tired and soon fell asleep.

When I awoke, I felt water on my face. I stood up and realized that I was in a rainstorm. It began raining harder and I was getting soaked. I looked around and could not see any other person. I was alone, just as I had hoped for!

I walked down the slope toward the base of the Bridge.

As I walked under the Bridge, I heard one loud clap of thunder! It shook the earth.

The sound coursed through me and I felt a great change enter my whole being. My mind was instantly opened to understand the things of God. All my feelings of darkness and evil left me. I instantly accepted the reality of God's being. I knew that his son was Jesus Christ, a person whose love extended out to me at this time of personal crisis. He was truly my Savior at that moment as all thoughts of my past trials faded and my heart was filled with wonder, compassion, peace and love.

I stood in the rain, not feeling cold or wet but feeling free from darkness and at peace. I was filled with a spirit of joy that words cannot describe. I did not see anyone; however, I felt a strong and powerful connection to God and his son, Jesus Christ. I remember feeling one with them and everything around me. It was as if our world was in perfect unison and everything was in order. God was at the helm.

I felt I was in the presence of a God of miracles as one was happening to me at that moment. God was alive! He communicated with me. He touched my heart and soul. I discovered miracles had not ceased, nor should they ever. I learned instantly about his existence and his son, Jesus Christ. The God of Abraham, Isaac and Jacob that I had learned about in the Jewish religion was the same God who I felt at that moment. This experience to me was sacred and wondrous. I was so grateful to God for helping me. I wept.

The Lord, Jesus Christ, gave me a new life. His spirit reached out to me in love and awakened in me a forgotten memory of who he was. I did not fully understand nor did I ask why this knowledge was given to me. I was content to feel a connection to God once again. I knew that this connection had always been there but the knowledge of him and his beloved son had been hidden or blocked. Now it was flowering and blooming and I wanted it to continue.

I did not want to leave this place, but I soon felt I must return to the boat. I reluctantly started down the path toward the excursion boat. I saw ahead of me two enormous waterfalls blocking my path. I also saw two men maneuvering their way under the waterfalls toward me. I recognized them from our boat. They had come looking for me. One of them took my hand and together we ducked under the large waterfall. I felt the sting of sand from the cascading water.

We all stopped and looked back at Rainbow Bridge. It was a magnificent sight standing as a testimony to me of what I had experienced there. The sun was coming out and I could see it reflected on every drop of rain as if I had a special curtain made up of rainbow colors framing the Bridge before me. Finally, the rain stopped and the curtain disappeared. I turned my back to the Bridge and walked to the boat. This experience was brief, but its effect on my life will last forever. (For the full story read "My Miracle from God.")

Since Rainbow Bridge

I have learned so much since that afternoon at Rainbow Bridge. I can tell you without any hesitation that God lives and he has a perfect plan for us and our world. Prayer and communication with God is active, on-going and needed.

I know that I am on a true spiritual journey as I walk the paths of mortal life. I continue to have trials but I now face them with the knowledge of God's purpose, as well as his son, Jesus Christ, to assist me and with a faithful husband at my side.

Need for Faith in God

There comes a time in our lives when we need God.

How much richer our lives can become when we extend our knowledge beyond this world and take the leap of faith forward into the Kingdom of God. How much greater is our hope in our future if we know that we are actually spirit children of God, his sons and daughters. Why only strive for the things of the world when there is a much greater hope that will come to us through our Savior, Jesus Christ, that will last forever?

Repentance from Sin is Essential

This is the time of repenting of our sins to see if we can become worthy to return home to our Father's house, for no unclean thing can dwell there. Why would we choose only the temporary riches of the earth when we can obtain the permanent riches of exaltation and eternal life? Real success in this life is a family and children filled with love for one another, who live gospel principles and are sealed or bound together as a family for all eternity.

Thanks to the Jewish People

The Jewish people suffered and died to bring the world both the Old and New Testaments. Through their lineage came our Savior, Jesus Christ, and many of the apostles. It was the Jews, the ancient covenant people of the Lord, who brought these scriptures and knowledge to the world. But what thanks have they been given by the Christian community? I have not given up my Jewish heritage. It is my foundation. But now I have the added knowledge that God lives, as does his son, Jesus Christ, who is the Messiah. I now understand their purpose. It all works together perfectly.

In the depths of my soul, I have often wondered who I am and desired to know the purpose of my being on earth. Now these things are opened to me, and this is pleasing to my spirit, which has sought light to fill the darkness of my limited understanding. The spirit within me is now peaceful, for I have found my God. The events of life and the promptings of the Lord have led me to my Savior, Jesus Christ, and his kingdom here on earth. Many do not yet know of the true nature of their Messiah, the fact that he has come and that he truly is the Savior of the world. One day all shall know, just as I now know.

The miracle of God that opened my mind, my soul and my heart happens to each of us in different ways as our needs arise. I needed a clap of thunder in a place called Rainbow Bridge. But you may gain a testimony that He lives in your own way and in your own time. This knowledge is confirmed to us by the Holy Ghost who tells us all truth, in a way we can understand. In every case, it is truly a miracle that occurs and changes our very nature. We gain an insight that extends beyond this world. These great truths can change our lives and give us happiness and hope for eternity.

I share my story with you as the first story in this book. I hope you will read the following short stories and use them to evaluate your belief in God and his son, Jesus Christ. The last story in this book is yours to complete for your own spiritual journey.

2 WHO AM I?

4 | THE SECRET

There once was an outstanding lady who kept her secrets locked in a drawer.
She had eyes of blue-green and hair like the flow of dreams.
She wore silk and chiffon and pearls that glowed against her fair skin.
Diamonds sparkled in her ears and her voice had the melody of faint violins.
Her smell was as sweet as lilac and her touch, the caress of angel's wings.
Her smile was warm and her spirit glowed like an eternal flame.
She was beauty to behold.

Her demure nature and chaste appearance always gave rise to speculation
about her secret.
Her strength and core of grace came through her commitment to God.
Her knowledge was enormous and her commitment sure and complete.
She was God's child and she knew it, for there was no secret hidden there.
How did she live beyond the doubt of the world?
How did she remain untouched and pure in spirit?
What was her secret?

She stood in the middle of a great hall surrounded by people all looking and
wanting to know her secret.
Each one coveted her calm assurance and envied her peace.
If only they could grab a small lock of hair,
Take a piece of her fine silk dress.
Surely if they just had a small token then they too could learn her secret.

They questioned her and prodded her.
They ogled and ignored her.
They hated her and called her insane.
They adored her and wept with her.

What was her secret?

Finally, she spoke.

From the melody of her voice, angels could be heard.
Her secret was out in the open for all to hear and understand.
Some people put their hands over their ears so they would not hear.

Others turned away and walked quickly through worldly doors that beckoned
    them.
A few remained and listened and learned.

Now they shared her secret.
Now they too understood.
They turned with tears in their eyes and a whisper in their voice.
The quiet words were said on bended knees.
Thank you, Heavenly Father, for our lives.
Thank you for your peace and comfort.
Thank you for your blessings.
We believe you now.

5 | THE BEAUTY OF SALVATION

There was a woman of great respect. She worked hard and employed many people in her business. She cared for her people and sought what was best for everyone. She was married once but that did not work out. Her children were grown and her first grandchild would be born in a few weeks.

Each night, she would go home, take off her shoes, and fix a meal. Then she would turn on the television to listen to the news. She was always amazed at the frightful scene of events that unfolded in front of her.

There were murders and the trials of murderers.
There were deaths through accidents.
There were wind storms, fire, drought and rain.
There were bodies lying in the streets.
There were nations collapsing due to violence and plague.
There were peace processes being diverted for personal gain.
There were people in the government arrested for wrongdoing.
All of this was brought into her home through her television set.

She turned the television off and settled back with her favorite book.
She read of things to come and their meaning.
She read of great civilizations long past that had been obliterated and disappeared.
She read of righteous men preaching to nations repentance or their great cities would be crushed.
She read of coming calamities and great forces battling for the souls of mankind.
She read of destruction and famine.
She read of betrayal and greed.
She read on and on and began to cry.

She had just heard all of this on the television, but the book she was reading was of ancient date. It was the Bible.

She sat there with her head bowed and asked God.
Will we ever learn?

6 | THE CHOCOLATE BAR

There was a soul that was empty. He tried to fill it up with chocolate bars and potato chips. The chocolate was the best. Then he added a little broccoli and carrots for vitamins. For lunch he ate a pasta salad, granola bar, hamburger, and French fries with ketchup; all of this in one day. What a mess. He took a handful of vitamins to offset the damage.

After work, he went to the gym to work out. Of course, this was the first time in months he went. He got on every machine and sweated for hours. When he left, he vowed to train more regularly instead of all at once. Now he was hungry again. He stopped by the quick Chinese place for some rice and Chinese vegetables to take home. He gulped it down in front of the television. Then he went to bed after midnight.

The next morning, he ran to get into his car and fight the traffic to get to work. On the way he picked up a donut and munched on it as he rode the elevator. Then he gulped down two cups of coffee and slid into his chair to work. He was on the phone, on the computer, down the hall, at a meeting, at his desk until late at night. He missed the gym again. Oh well, maybe tomorrow.

Four years passed by. He looked at his calendar one day and said. "What happened? I remember when I went to the gym four years ago. I have it marked right here." He noticed that his shoe was untied so he tried to bend over his large belly to get to his shoe, but it was too difficult. He would have to buy loafers instead. What was he going to do? He was not married. He ate the wrong food. He never exercised. He had no life. He was just an eating machine that talked on the phone and did his job.

Was this his life? I guess it was. He wondered what he was missing.

The camera zoomed out of his office, outside the window, up into the heavens. God looked down upon his people and saw thousands sitting at their desks munching chocolate bars and potato chips. He saw all the empty souls trying to fill themselves up. When would they learn that food alone was not enough? Work alone was not enough.

When would they figure it out?

When would they fill themselves with faith, repentance and righteousness? Only these will fill an empty soul.

7 | Unwrap the Package

There was a time upon the earth when the precious package of mankind was created.

Unwrap the package and open the veil of tissue that covers our true beginning and the nature of God within us.

Open the package and allow yourselves to receive the gifts from God that will unlock the doors to spiritual understanding.

Don't let others untie the knots. They must be untied by your own faith.

Whosoever depends upon another for divine intervention has unfolded the package in darkness.

Open the package and peel back each and every layer until the pieces lay all around you.

Unwrap the layer of doubt and throw it out.

Unwrap the layer of hatred and throw it into the fire.

Unwrap the layer of jealousy and greed and shred it so that it is unrecognizable.

Unwrap the tissue of life and open the portals of understanding that is God.

Unwrap the last layer and grow in understanding and truth.

Unwrap all the layers, peel away the dark edges and add the new tissue of life into a re-formed and newly cleansed package.

8 | THE LIVING GOSPEL

What is the gospel of Jesus Christ and does it now live upon this earth in the hearts and minds of mankind?

What did Jesus Christ have in mind when man was created?

Was it necessary to have a plan of salvation?

Aren't we here just to live in this world and then turn to dust?

The tragic formula that people use to live in this world combines desperation, overwork, chaos and emptiness. Then we mix in small glimpses of joy and love in between a mountain of decisions. Then we have the modern-day sandwich of life. Every once in a while, a little mayonnaise is added to grease the wheels. We are so busy with exacting out a living and paying the bills that there is little time for prayer and true reflection.

Then how do we proclaim the gospel of Jesus Christ and how can it help us in our lives?

The gospel is the truth: the truth about our value as a human being and our potential. Our spiritual awareness can lead us out of the chaos of the up and down natures of our lives into smoother-flowing streams and byways.

Picture this: You are in a raft floating down the river. The water is smooth and you can see the rocks beneath the surface. Suddenly you can see the water churning and the rapids foaming. You will have to traverse those rapids, but you have faith that you are safe in the raft. All the provisions and knowledge are in the raft with you. There is nothing that has been omitted. You are scared, for you doubt your ability to maneuver through the rapidly moving water. These doubts enter your mind and your gut. But then you row ahead and suddenly you are in the clear. You exclaim, that was not so bad.

But you had to prepare. You needed the right provisions. You needed the raft and all the equipment. You knew the basics, and therefore were successful when the waters were not smooth.

So it is with the gospel of Jesus Christ. When you understand the true and full gospel of Jesus Christ and then attempt to live as God commands, then you will have the knowledge and faith needed when the smooth waters turn rough, for you know that in the end they will smooth out for your blessing.

9 | CONNECTED

Who are you?

That is the question. Whether it is nobler to bear the slings and arrows of hate-filled words is your choice. Whether to look forward to a future of love and caring could be your choice. Whether to work hard and form a partnership with God is your decision. Whether to stop your whining and complaining and do something with your life to help others is up to you.

But that is only the first part.

The second part concerns your decisions and how these affect others. Who you are can also be defined by the people around you—how you treat them, how you interact with them, how you love and serve them.

Who are you?

This question has been asked by so many people that God must be tired of hearing it. The answer is, we are his children. We can start from there. That would be a good beginning.

Then, where do we go from there?

We live in an organized world, established by the physical and natural laws now in place. We work in an organized environment. The world becomes chaos after we set into motion the wrong choices, feelings, thoughts and actions. From this start, a circle of influence begins and spreads out amongst God's people in an ever increasing crescendo of trauma. Then it takes at least one, but most likely many people, to stop the tide of evil that sweeps across the plains of the planet. How many times does peace come in the form of heroic men and women standing firm to stop the evil? How many times does comfort come in the form of others reaching out and caring? How many volunteers show up when tragedy strikes?

What if each person who participated in either the violent behavior or the peace process knew that they were being judged on their performance as a human being? Who would be the judge of us all? God? Jesus Christ? Other people? Our families and friends? Who? Why should we care?

What if this were true? What if everything that you did, every thought, and every word was part of the watchwords of your life? What if, after death, you had to answer for everything that you did or said and how it affected others? If you were responsible for the lives of others through your words, would you be more careful?

How do you feel now? Who are you? Are you responsible for all your brothers and sisters? Are you being judged by only your lies, only your actions, only your love? Are you being judged by how you have helped others? Are you being judged at all? But if you are subject to a larger judgment than is on this earth, what then? How would you react?

What if I told you that God exists, Jesus Christ exists, and the Holy Spirit exists and that you should live by the laws of God. Would you try harder? Many already are trying and live righteous lives. That does not mean we are perfect. We are not. But through the atonement of Christ, we can be made perfect in the eyes of God. Isn't that what we should strive for?

Let's start at the beginning and consider the source. God exists and rules his universe. You are God's spirit children. You are subject to the laws set in place by God for this world and the world beyond. Can you fathom our responsibility to each other and to God? Why do you think that the greatest commandment of God is to love the Lord thy God with all thy heart, and with all thy soul, and with all thy mind; and to love thy neighbor as thyself. What else could this mean? Why, above all else are these the greatest commandments?

Who are you? Please think about your own lives and how you are affected by the words of others. Are you happy when someone around you is happy? Are you sad when you see pain and suffering? Do you treat others in a way that is consistent with the way you feel? How does that affect them? When you walk into an office with a smile on your face and say hello to everyone, does the whole office seem lighter and the people get along better? When you walk into an office and you are sullen and distracted, do people avoid you? It is as if they do not want to feel the way you do, so they stay away. Your mood might be contagious. If you are hard on your employees, do you think they go home and take it out on their families? How many people do you think you affect?

Are we all connected?

Can we even begin to watch our words and slow down our speech patterns? This is very hard. But when we think of the reverberations that it causes, then it might help us to consider our words, our actions and our reactions. It is hard and will take a lot of work, but we can try.

What do you think? Is it worth a try? Who are you?

Only you and your Heavenly Father know.

3

THE RIGHT PATH

10 | THE RIGHT PATH

The miracle was his life. He had been at war in a country far away. He flew overseas with his platoon and then returned alive with his whole body intact. That was the miracle. The place was strewn with land mines like rows of potatoes. Didn't the army think that they might have to walk upon the same ground again? It was like a spider web. If you step here, maybe you will live and maybe not. They did not care who stepped into the plowed field or what happened. All they wanted to do was to maim and hurt.

One day, the platoon leader said. "No one will walk into that plowed field until a map is made."

This map would take a long time because every mine had to be found so no one would step on it and be harmed. The process was slow because no one wanted to make a mistake—one error and you could lose a limb or life. The plan was to provide a safe path across the minefield to the other side. Once the map was made, then it was a matter of following the rules and the right path. After many days, the map was finished.

The first man said, "I will cross. I have faith that you found all the mines and I will make it across to safety." So he went. He carefully followed the path on the map and made it to the other side.

Then the next man went along the same path and was also safe. Many followed along later. Soon the path got a little messy. The tenth man in line thought he knew how to cross, but he tripped. He just ran onto the path and didn't take the time to learn the correct route. The results were not nice.

Then the fiftieth man got tired and decided to rest in the middle of the field. So, he sat down. The path was too narrow so he too had a problem.

Then the hundredth man carefully watched every foot and heard every sound. He took a very long time to get across but he finally made it. He was just elderly when he finished.

The thousandth man forgot that there was a map at all. He looked at the abandoned field and desperately wanted to get to the other side. It just looked like a harmless field. He did not notice the roped off areas with signs saying, "Do not enter." He walked across, oblivious to the warnings, and did not make it.

The ten-thousandth man sat at the edge of the field and decided that he better find someone to tell him about this field so he would not end up dead. He knew that he had to find the map, so he went in search of the answer and finally located the original document. "Oh," he said. "Now I know how to get across safely." So, he started walking.

What about eternal life and exaltation? Do you need a map to get there? Yes. If we want safety, we all need help from a truthful source.

11 | THE EAGLE SOARED

Far off into the sky, I spotted an eagle soaring above the winding path in the canyon. I stood up and caught a fleeting glimpse of this magnificent bird as she carried food to her children. I saw the eagle land on a ledge high above the valley.

The eagle listened to her young as they ate. They wanted to fly, but they were not ready yet. They moved around and flapped their wings but stayed in place all the same.

The young birds cried out. "When will we be ready to fly? When? When?"

The mother looked at them from side to side and up and down. "Soon," she said. "Soon. You do not have enough knowledge yet."

They pleaded with her to teach them.

She said, "That is your father's job. Ask him."

The father soared down and landed elegantly next to his family. He heard their complaints and their wishes. He heard their wants and desires. They were hungry, even though they had just eaten. They wanted to fly and wanted to know how. They wanted this information now!

Their father said, "There is much to learn. We will start at the beginning."

So they listened and learned. They questioned, they repeated. They understood. But could they fly? As the weeks went by they memorized. They recited. They ate and became stronger. They flapped their wings.

Then one day their father landed near them and said, "It is time to fly."

They looked at him and fear entered their minds. Could they remember all the lessons? Could they do it?

Their father said to them, "Learning is not just memorizing and repeating. It is a process of understanding and growth. It is necessary that you learn to use what you have been taught. What good would you be if you stayed in the nest and never flew? Mother and I will not feed you forever. You must learn to fly and provide for yourselves. But we will always be here to help you when you fall until you grow strong enough to fly. Help others and teach them also."

So the little birds walked up to the ledge, each repeating in their heads their lessons. Suddenly all was quiet. It was time to implement and live their knowledge. They had to have faith they could fly.

They stepped off the cliff and soared in majesty like their father and mother.

12 | THE MYSTERY OF GOD

Who is God?

There is a mystery surrounding the existence of God. This started when man decided that his logic was much better than God's. Man knew the truth when focused on the discoveries of science. He would only believe what was in front of him. He would only conceive of what could be measured, charted and scientifically proven. But what is a known fact today changes tomorrow when more scientific discoveries are made. So, what is the truth?

When you delve into the unknown and find something brand new, does this new conclusion change your mind from what you knew before?

How can you say that you will only believe what you see, when you don't know from second to second what new invention might be announced or new knowledge discovered?

What is the mystery of God? Think about the poetry of life and the music of emotions. Think about the discoveries for the good of mankind and the evolution of thought. Think about the processes of nature and its perfect structure and organization. Can you conceive of even your own body? God can.

What is the mystery of God? Can you stop time or measure the true speed of existence? Can you measure a moment or equate your beginnings to your scientific logic? Can you comprehend eternity and the magnitude of the universe?

What is the mystery of God? What do people mean when they feel the peace and calm of the Holy Spirit? What do people know when the physical weight of a sin has been lifted off their shoulders through repentance and faith in Jesus Christ? Why do people pray to God, and are their prayers answered? Why are there so many people who believe that God exists?

You may not have even taken the time to consider the possibility. Why don't you have the answers to everything on this earth if you are so smart? Haven't you had enough time to figure it out?

What is the mystery of God?
There is no mystery.
He just is and can help us if we ask in faith.

13 | "OH GOD"

"Oh, my God" she exclaimed! "For God's sake, don't let this happen to me." She implored God in a way that she knew how, but this time she was really trying to talk to God.

Carol was a casual girl. She worked hard at her job in the videotaping division of the television news department. She was in charge of the final product before it was shown on television. Every day she came to work, not knowing what the latest tragedy would be. She watched the video and corrected or shortened it to fit the new schedule. Was the news too long or too short? Was it too wordy or, just right? She edited, fixed and then timed it to fit its slot. Every time she had a glitch she said, "Oh, God!" She used this term a lot as if it had no meaning at all. It was just something to say when she got frustrated. Then when she was really mad or upset with someone or a situation, she would say, "Jesus Christ!" These terms were as common to her as "hello." She said them without thinking.

But one day a tape came in from a major highway accident. It had just happened and the people involved were so mangled she could not see who they were. As usual, she started the video and her timer. She was glancing away, but something caught her eye. It was the car. Her husband had one just like it. She looked closer and then saw the license plate. It was her husband's car. She sat stunned in front of the machine as the video played on. Its dispassionate resonance echoed in her mind. "Oh God!" she said with tears streaming down her cheeks.

"No, please God, NO!" Who was this God she was talking to? The one so casually dismissed before or the one she asked help from? She found the crew that filmed the accident to find out what happened to the people inside. They were killed—crushed inside of their car.

"They?" she said. "One of them was my husband."

"Oh, God," they said. "We are so sorry."

But who else was killed? They did not know, but there was another person—a woman. Carol talked further with them and found out where her husband was taken.

She walked into the darkened corridor toward the area where the bodies were located. She saw her husband first and then the other person. Who was she? Someone he worked with? How did the accident happen? All sorts of thoughts coursed through her mind—unwanted thoughts. The police officer approached her and asked her quietly to identify herself. After looking at her intently, he told her that her husband was a victim of a drive-by shooting. The killer, unknown, was long gone. The woman was not in her husband's car, but was actually driving the car next to him. Both cars careened off the road and landed in a heap at the bottom of a hill. Both people were killed instantly. The woman was married with two young children.

It was just one of those everyday deaths that she saw on the video. One of those common occurrences she had gotten used to seeing. She had seen so many that she had become numb. But why her husband? He was such a good man and now it was too late for him to live his life.

"Oh, God!" she moaned, not thinking about the meaning of her statement. "Oh, God."

14 | THE GLORY OF GOD

The Kingdom of Heaven is open to you now.

The glory of Jesus Christ is known, for he came to earth and freed us from our sins if we will repent.

Behold the King of Kings.

Behold the glory of God.

Sing his praises and humble yourselves before him in reverence and supplication.

Kneel down in respect for the Lord our God that loves you all so much that he offers you the gift of life eternal.

It is there for the taking.

It is in front of your eyes, but it is hard to see.

It is discussed and told to you in an endless array of words, but you do not hear.

Why are you so blinded to the light that is shining before you?

Why would you reject such a wonderful gift?

This gift comes with the springtime of renewal.

This gift comes with the everlasting life that you seek.

This gift comes with no lies or deception.

If you deviate from the laws of God, then you can repent and change.

If you make a commitment and strive for the better life that God intended, then you will be fulfilled.

If you study and live the life of love that God envisions, then you defeat all the doubts, fears and hatreds in the world.

If you have faith that God is real and you live by the gospel of Jesus Christ, then God's blessings will be known to you and your life will improve.

If you pray to God and ask for the truth of your own nature as a human being, then be ready for some answers from Him.

If you get the answers, what then?

Will you believe what you hear?

If you do, then a whole world will be opened up to you and you will no longer suffer doubts of mind.

What is the great faith of the people of God?

What is the triumphant battle song that will break apart the shackles that bind us?

What would it be like on earth if everyone tried to live by the gospel of Jesus Christ?

It would be heaven on earth.

Would you rather have Heaven or Hell, either now or later?

15 | THE CREATION

The formation of the land mass came together and then separated. It crashed and then subsided. It formed new mountains and then separated into oceans. It sounded with great trumpet blasts and hissed as lava flowed forth.

Seeds were planted in the new ground and plants, fruits, and all kinds of vegetables started to grow. Trees formed halos above the new land and you could hear the animals as they sang their various refrains.

The earth molded together and brought forth its bounty. The earth grew and changed. Color was added as if by a paintbrush dipped in God's colors. Odors sweet as honey and scents of pine could be smelled. Herbs and spices of all varieties grew and became abundant. Delicious fruit and enticing flowers blossomed. Birds sang their sweet songs. Lakes of water rippled in the wind. Mountains of glory rose steep and tall. Animals stepped lively and munched on the fine grasses.

The rains began and replenished the earth and everything grew. The soft and gentle breezes made a sound through the leaves of the trees. All was ready. The earth was a world of beauty and abundance.

"Ah," God said. "It is good. Let us put man upon the earth." So it began.

Let's use it for God's glory.

16 | THE NOBLE HOUSE

There was a Noble House of the Lord. The Lord was the wisest in the region and knew his responsibility was great. He listened to his people and made his decisions with great wisdom. His esteem was large, for his virtue was well known and his fairness always apparent. He loved his people.

His laws became a way of life. People were happy in their work. His wisdom came from seeking the good in others. His thoughts were of a higher and nobler dimension. His demeanor was somber at times, but mostly he smiled and laughed with those he worked with. He was saddened when people would not let him help. If that happened, he wiped away the tears and disappointment and went on to other work and other people.

Then one day a visitor appeared and tore down his house with words of censure, criticism and calamity.

The visitor said, "Life is too good and too many people are happy. This is not the way of the world. Look at the disease, decay and destruction. Look at the killings, earthquakes and famine. Change your lives, people of this kingdom, for the Noble Lord has deceived you into believing that life is happy, quiet and filled with love and peace. Wake up to the 'real' world and be deceived no more."

The Noble Lord was appalled at the words of this visitor.

The peace his people long enjoyed was splintered by the pain the visitor foretold, because they believed him. They began to hide away in fear of each other and lock their minds.

The Noble Lord pleaded with them to look again and see the true value of their lives with each other and with him, to remember the way it was just a short while ago.

The people grumbled, for they saw the riches of others and coveted them. They saw the clothes and fine jewelry and sought them and the vices of the World. They forgot that they already possessed everything. Now, they hoarded and stockpiled. They amassed great fortunes and built walls around their houses and their lives. They forgot to ask the Noble Lord to help them find the better answer. They thought they knew it all.

Suddenly, everything stopped and all was quiet, for the people began to shake and shimmer. Their form vanished and re-emerged. They could not focus on each other for they became shapeless and without substance. They became only the clothes and jewelry. The emptiness became complete, for the clothes contained a human without form or substance.

Soon tears started leaking from the eyes of the people. Their hearts began to open and they began to remember the time of the Noble Lord when wisdom and love were the standard and all lived together in peace.

What happened? Where had they lost this former time that was so precious? Many sat together and talked of life remembered, of security, safety and love. They remembered that sanctuary must come from the Lord God, the Noblest House of them all and by following his standards.

Seek and ye shall find. Remember the Lord God again.

17 | BE ONE

Be calm, my spirit, for I seek the path of the Lord.

Be quiet, my spirit, for God speaks in a whisper.

Be alert, my spirit, for false pride, jealousy and greed knock at my door.

Be brave, my spirit, for my strength comes from the Lord, and there is nothing to fear.

Be strong, my spirit, for the battle rages and we are victorious.

Be one in purpose, my spirit, with God, Jesus Christ and the Holy Spirit.

18 | COME TO GOD

There was a short time upon the earth when God and mankind lived together in peace. God's people loved him and worshiped him. There was a short time in the framework of mankind that God and man coexisted in total understanding and harmony.

Then the devil brought upon this earth the doubt and greed of evil. He wanted God's children to worship him. He lulled them into complacency and disuse. He used the gold and glitter of the universe to entice them. If they gave him their agency, he eventually controlled their minds and bodies. He punished them for their faith in God. He whispered the blame was on God instead of himself, and stood back and laughed at their reluctance to continue in the truth of the Deliverer.

He who does not understand is truly lost, for the playing field of life is changing. The patterns will be harder and harder to maintain. The insolence of God's children has hardened into the immorality and unbelief that exists upon the earth now.

How empty your lives have become.

Why do you do this when God can give you so much?

Why do you cast aside God's gifts as if they are of no value?

Why do you cheat yourselves out of God's love and salvation through his son, Jesus Christ?

How sorry you have become, for you run around in circles, joining and talking, but the truth of your former spiritual power is hidden from you.

Come to God in supplication and ask for the return of your birthright as one of God's children upon this earth.

Come to God in worship as you describe your needs.

Come to God in worship, for he is your Lord and you are his child.

Come to God through his son, Jesus Christ, who went through so much trauma and pain to free you from your sins, if you repent.

Come to God before it is too late. Listen to God's Wake-Up Call.

19 | THE LAWS OF GOD

There was a people of God united in the song of life. They worshiped and adored him. They spoke in hushed tones and prayed in the quiet of their rooms. Their God had given them a set of laws by which to live. Each law was simply stated and could be understood by everyone. They were not hard laws to follow, for the rewards were so great when they did. Why wouldn't they want to continue within the blessed shelter of God?

They wrote the laws of God on a great wall in the City so that everyone could see them at all times of the day or night. These are great laws and no one could dispute them.

The people lived within great prosperity and love. They produced much more than they needed so they sought the outside world to share their wealth.

As the traders passed through other areas outside of their country, they noticed that those they met lived and did business differently. The outsiders could not be trusted. They did not love, care or respect one another. They worshiped graven images. Some worshiped golden gods with sapphire eyes, some worshiped wooden totem poles, some worshiped kings and men, and some worshiped animals. How could these people worship these things made by the hands of mankind? When the traders inquired about this, they were told that they needed a reminder to worship their god. They needed an image. They needed something they could hold in their hands and feel and touch. They needed someone to set up rituals and habits by which to worship. They needed a strict structure so that they would know at all times what was required of them to appease their god. The trader tried to explain his concept of God and Jesus Christ. They would not listen. They did not want to understand.

The traders were appalled. When they received their goods, they were of poor quality and never the right amount ordered.

When they inquired of these errors, they were told, "Well, that is how we do business. We try and catch each other in our mistakes and errors so that we can argue about it. We can then raise our voices and yell at each other. It is fun. That is what we do."

"But," the traders said, "What about the right way to do business?"

The outsiders replied, "We just don't work that way at all. We prefer to live with deceit and a vague sense of the purpose of life." They were not certain about this, but they thought that was how it always was in their country.

The traders returned home to find peace and order, love and harmony. They wanted to build a strong wall of faith around the people of God so that outsiders would not get in with their horrible vices. But this did not happen. As trade with outsiders increased then objects of worship started to abound within the land.

Those who could see what was happening said, "No. Do not change what you do and how you live. Look at the great wall of God's laws and live righteously. Do not worship the things made by man. Do not worship other men. There is only one God to worship through his son, Jesus Christ. Through the teachings of Jesus Christ, you can receive salvation."

But the people decided that they preferred to build large edifices and place within them their version of God. They bowed down and sang praises to their king in the flesh, but not the King of Kings. The peace began to be shattered with arguments and deception. The world changed and the people forgot the great laws of God. Great wars broke out and many died.

It was not convenient to look upon the wall anymore. They could do what they wanted. And they did.

The wall was eventually torn down and the people erected great courts of law that tried to dispense justice. They erected great jails to incarcerate the people who broke the new laws of the land. But whose laws remained now? The people forgot about God and continued to ply their trades and live their lives. They were in charge and they yelled their rights out loud.

Then one day, the earth shook and the waters of the flood came upon all that were there. The people drowned and the idols sank to the bottom of the sea. The earth was washed clean again.

Noah, his family and animals departed from the ark. The first thing they did was to re-erect the wall of God's laws. The earth became fruitful again and multiplied. Abundance and prosperity filled the houses of the great Lord. After a time, they decided to find other people to trade with. And then it began again.

THE LAWS WRITTEN UPON THE WALL OF GOD

1. Worship God
   - Thou shalt love the Lord thy God with all thine heart, and with all thy soul, and with all thy might.
   - Thou shalt have no other gods before me.
   - Thou shalt not make unto thee any graven image, or any likeness of anything that is in heaven above, that is the earth beneath, or that is in the water under the earth.
   - Thou shalt not bow down thyself to them, nor serve them.
   - Thou shalt not take the name of the Lord thy God in vain; for the Lord will not hold him guiltless that taketh his name in vain.
   - Ye shall not make gods of sliver, neither shall ye make unto you gods of gold:
   - No man can serve two masters: for either he will hate the one and love the other; or else he will hold to the one, and despise the other. Ye cannot serve God and Mammon.

2. Fellow Men, Family
   - Honour thy father and thy mother: that thy days may be long upon the land which the Lord thy God giveth thee.
   - Give to him that asketh thee, and from him that would borrow of thee turn not thou away.
   - Judge not, that ye be not judged. For with what judgment ye judge, ye shall be judged: and with that measure ye mete, it shall be measured to you again.
   - Thou shalt love thy neighbour as thyself.

3. Sexual Immorality
   - Thou shalt not commit adultery, nor do anything like unto it.
   - Thou shalt not commit adultery: Whosever looketh on a woman to lust after her hath committed adultery with her already in his heart.
   - But if thine eye be evil, thy whole body shall be full of darkness. If therefore the light that is in thee be darkness, how great is that darkness.

4. Pride
   - When thou prayest, thou shalt not be as the hypocrites are: for they love to pray standing in the synagogues and in the corners of the streets, that they may be seen of men. But thou, when thou prayest, enter into thy closet, and when thou hast shut thy door, pray to thy Father which is in secret and thy Father which seeth in secret shall reward thee openly.
   - When ye pray, use not vain repetitions, as the heathen do: for they think that they shall be heard for their much speaking. Be not ye therefore like unto them: for your Father knoweth what things ye have need of, before ye ask him.

5. Repentance
   - Repent, for the kingdom of heaven is at hand.
   - Preach the baptism of repentance, for the remission of sins.
   - Joy shall be in heaven over one sinner that repenteth.

6. God's Blessings
   - And shewing mercy unto thousands of them that love me, and keep my commandments.
   - The light of the body is the eye: if therefore thine eye be single, thy whole body shall be full of light.
   - Seek ye first the kingdom of God, and his righteousness; and all these things shall be added unto you.
   - Enter ye in at the strait gate: for wide is the gate, and broad is the way, that leadeth to destruction, and many there be which go in thereat: Because strait is the gate, and narrow is the way, which leadeth unto life, and few there be that find it.
   - Therefore whosoever heareth these sayings of mine, and doeth them, I will liken him unto a wise man, which built his house upon a rock.
   - Let your light so shine before men, that they may see your good works, and glorify your Father which is in heaven.

7. Sabbath Day
   - Remember the sabbath day, to keep it holy.
   - Six days shalt thou labour, and do all thy work.

- But the seventh day is the sabbath of the Lord thy God: in it thou shalt not do any work, thou, nor thy son, nor thy daughter, thy manservant, nor thy maidservant, nor thy cattle, nor thy stranger that is within thy gates.
- For in six days the Lord made heaven and earth, the sea, and all that in them is, and rested the seventh day: wherefore the Lord blessed the sabbath day, and hallowed it.

8. Lie, Steal, Anger, Murder
    - Thou shalt not kill.
    - Thou shalt not steal.
    - Thou shalt not bear false witness against thy neighbor.
    - Thou shalt not covet thy neighbour's house, thou shalt not covet thy neighbour's wife, nor his manservant, nor his maidservant, nor his ox, nor his ass, nor anything that is thy neighbour's.
    - Thou shalt not kill; whosoever shall kill shall be in danger of the judgment:
    - Whosoever is angry with his brother without a cause shall be in danger of the judgment.
    - Agree with thine adversary quickly, whiles thou art in the way with him; lest at any time thy adversary deliver thee to the judge, and the judge deliver thee to the officer, and thou be cast into prison. Thou shalt by no means come out thence, till thou has paid the uttermost farthing.
    - Beware of false prophets, which come to you in sheep's clothing, but inwardly they are ravening wolves.
    - Swear not at all; neither by heaven; for it is God's throne: Nor by the earth; for it is his footstool.

9. Persecution
    - Love your enemies, bless them that curse you, do good to them that hate you, and pray for them which despitefully use you, and persecute you.

20 | THE MOUNTAIN OF LIFE

There was a mountain of life,
Tall and strong,
Filled with the strength of Jesus Christ,
Filled with his courage, his love and his service to all mankind.

Find your way through the labyrinth of life that is now on this earth and
search for the truth.
Find the way to God through Jesus Christ's commandments to us all.
Find your own strength and vision through the whispering of the Holy Spirit.
Find the answers to all the ennobling questions you seek.

Add to your lives the love of God, for it is there to take.
Reach out your heart to God and find a fulfillment that only he can give you
through your righteousness.
Believe in the hope of the world who is Jesus Christ.

Become a mountain of spiritual strength through your faith and commitment
to the living God.
Know that his words still live upon this earth through God's true prophets
and apostles.
Know that God's judgments of your life include his mercy.
Know that all destruction must cease and all hatred end.

Step through your wall of blindness and seek the love of God.
Know that you are a spirit and a body and choose for yourselves to become
what God intended.
Know that you can change, for with each act of kindness comes great
fulfillment.

Seek and ye shall find.
Knock and the door will open.

21 | LIVING WATERS

The river flows onward into the hills and the valleys below. The water continues in a never-ending cycle of life and death—life as the water gives and death in its absence.

So likewise is the spirit—ever flowing, always moving through every pore of your bodies, cleansing, washing, and directing your thirst for the things of God.

The water of eternal life is like the river, ever flowing. It can cover you and bring you death or renew your life through baptism and remission of sin. The waters of life fill to overflowing through Christ, your Lord.

So why is looking at a flowing river important? It mesmerizes, intrigues, and brings peace into your heart. It can remind you of the pattern of life as it ebbs and flows in different ways.

Look at the river. It is constant in its flow but the patterns shift every moment—just like life. One moment can be great and the next not. But just as the river continues onwards, so does your life, always moving forward into a new realm, always a new beginning.

The key is to see beyond the vision before your eyes into a new dimension. Where does the river end? Is it into a great ocean or a desert that will absorb all its moisture?

Is your view of vast new horizons or can you not see beyond what is in front of you?

Now look from above as the Lord sees and see the vast rivers of living waters as they reach toward his children. The pattern of the water is ever flowing, shifting and seeking new openings.

Look beyond the river into the Kingdom of God where living waters flow for eternity.

Look to your Savior, Jesus Christ.

4
SOLUTIONS UNLOCKED

22 | THE KEY

Every time Mona went home, she slammed the door. Her father said, "Hey Mona, why do you always slam the door? Do you want to break it? Huh? I have already replaced the hinges and oiled the hasps. I have repaired the wood frame and hammered the nails back into place. Why can't you gently close the door?"

"Well, Father," Mona said, "How else would you know I was home? Some days I slam it because I am so mad and it helps me get rid of my rage. Other days I am in a hurry and don't want to take the time to close it softly. I can be halfway up the stairs in the time it takes to do that. Then other days, I just want everyone to know it's me. I am home! So that is why I slam the door."

Her father looked at her and shook his head. "Oh Mona, won't you ever learn that you need to consider how others feel about this also?"

Mona would not listen. She ran up the stairs, changed, ran down the stairs and slammed the door on her way out.

When she returned home, the door was missing. There was no door to the house at all, only a blank wall. She stopped in front of the house and looked to make sure she was in the right place. Where was the door opening? How could she get inside the house? She walked all the way around and searched every inch of the house. There was no door opening.

She said, "Is this my house?" The address was right. So was the color and shape of the house. Now what, she thought. I need to change clothes. I have homework and then Monica is coming by to pick me up for a party tonight. This is really inconvenient.

She went up to the front and banged on the wall. "Let me in," she yelled. "Is anybody home?" No one answered. She looked for some windows, but they were all shuttered. There was one open window on the second floor. So she tried to yell. "HEY! Is anyone home?" No answer.

She was tired and tried to figure out what was happening. The whole neighborhood looked the same way. None of the houses had doors. She yelled and jumped up and down.

She sat on the stoop and thought about her father's words. She had never listened before. She did what she wanted no matter how many times he tried to talk to her. Maybe she was wrong. Maybe she should start listening.

Soon a car drove up. Her father got out of the car. She ran to him and gave him a huge hug and smile of relief. "Father, I should have listened to you. I can't find the door to our home. Can you help?"

"Sure," he said. "Here is the key."

Written on it were the words "REPENT and CHANGE!"

23 | THE RASPBERRY SUNDAE

Once there was an ice cream parlor. It was filled with all the flavors we love: chocolate, vanilla, strawberry and peach. It had sundaes and malts, cones and other concoctions. All kinds of condiments could be added. You could select pecans and walnuts, bananas and hot fudge. Just to look inside brought back dreams of childhood summers sitting on a tall stool in front of a counter loaded up with all kinds of treats.

But the best of all the sundaes was raspberry.

The owner had a raspberry bush behind his house and he picked fresh berries each day. He walked in with a bucket of raspberries and sweetened them just a little with sugar. Then he started a batch of homemade vanilla ice cream. We all watched as he made the ice cream. We could see the raspberries waiting and our mouths just watered.

We'd say, "Is it ready yet?"

And he'd say, "You are just going to have to be patient."

So we waited and waited until we just couldn't wait any longer and we'd say, "Is it ready yet?"

And he'd say, "No! You need to be patient."

Finally, the motor in the ice cream machine stopped and it was ready!

The owner took a clean wide cup and filled it with vanilla ice cream and topped it with fresh raspberries. The taste hit our tongue first and then our senses. How extraordinary—creamy, sweet and tart. No extra whipping cream was added. It was just perfect in its original form.

It was certainly worth the wait.

Patience is a virtue that must be learned, for many of our eternal rewards and God's blessings come later.

24 | THE SPLIT

Connie and Mike were sharing a banana split. It was made the new way with rocky road, French vanilla bean and strawberry shortcake ice cream. For toppings, they had hot fudge, marshmallow and caramel, in that order. Of course, whipped cream and a cherry were added on top as a final touch.

They had one bowl and two spoons. Connie liked to mix the marshmallow with rocky road so she reached over and took a scoop of the marshmallow and rocky road and mixed them together.

Mike was a puritan and ate exactly, in the same order, what was on top of each scoop of ice cream. Mike complained, "Connie, you are messing up the banana split. You shouldn't mix it all together. That is why it is called a 'banana split'—each group is a separate sundae."

Connie smiled while she was chewing and said, "Well, they should have poured the marshmallow over the rocky road ice cream. There are already marshmallows in the ice cream so they go together. Don't they know anything?"

Mike sighed. Oh well. It was so delicious; he could stand this for a short time. So they continued eating in silence.

Connie wanted to tease Mike, but he was not happy, so she went back to her side of the dish and ate in silence.

After a while, there was just a little of each left. Mike, with a twinkle in his eye, reached in and took a scoop of marshmallow and put it on Cindy's ice cream. "Wait!" she said, laughing. "You are mixing them."

She took some hot fudge and put it on his strawberry ice cream. He tasted it and decided it wasn't bad to be a little flexible. After all, everything wasn't just plain vanilla.

It was better to see Cindy smile and chatter than be split apart in silence. It was better to be flexible and look for value in other people's ideas.

25 | HE CARED

There was a rabbit, soft and white. It hopped around in a circle, crinkling its nose and looking everywhere. What was he searching for? For an instant, he glanced up and saw me. Suddenly he hopped over and pushed my foot with his nose. How sweet, I thought, just a cute little bunny rabbit. He rubbed his nose and sat up on his hind legs ready to listen. His ears perked up and his eyes looked at me expectantly and with great yearning. What could I possibly say or do for this bunny? He was so pretty and gentle, so kind to come over and keep me company. How did he know I was lonely?

I had never heard of a rabbit being friendly. I always saw them hopping away in fright. This one just seemed to be here for me. Do you suppose he could tell I just needed someone, anyone, to comfort me and to distract me from my depression? Such a little thing, but to me it was a miracle. The rabbit brushed my leg with his paw and again sat up and waited for me.

This is truly a miracle, I thought. I wonder if God could hear my pain and sent me this beautiful bunny to let me know I am really not alone.

As I sat there in the quiet of the park with this rabbit huddled close to my foot, I thanked God for his kind and gentle way of sending one of his creations to let me know he was listening and he cared.

Thank you, God.

26 | AUTUMN LEAVES

The wind was chilly. I wrapped my arms around my body to help keep me warm. The weather had suddenly changed and I was not dressed appropriately. As I walked home from school, I could smell the autumn air. It smelled clean and crisp. The leaves crinkled underneath my feet. I saw a pile of leaves and took a great run and leaped in. What fun! I laughed as I freed myself from the pile of leaves and continued walking.

I came across a tree that had already shed its leaves. How empty and alone it looked. All these other trees still had their beauty. I wondered if people ever felt like that tree. Some are plain on the outside but can blossom later.

I continued to walk. I saw a few dandelions standing alone in a field. Their yellow color collided with the green and brown surrounding them. They stood out in the field of grass and weeds. I wonder if people are like that. Some stand up for what they believe, but the majority just blend in.

I looked around again and saw to my surprise, our neighbor, old Mrs. Devers, raking her leaves and whistling. She had on an old grey sweater and corduroy pants. She also had on work boots and a warm cap. "Hi Mrs. Devers," I said. "May I jump into that pile of leaves you are making?"

"No," she said. "You can't. It will scatter them too much. But you could help me load them into these bags, if you have time."

"Sure," I said. "Let me call my mom and tell her I will be late." So I ran into her home and called my mom.

On my way out, I noticed all the pictures she had on the walls and tables. They were pictures of her husband and kids. She had five grown children and fourteen grandchildren. She also had two great-grandchildren. There were pictures everywhere. Her kids lived nearby. I wondered why they didn't come over and help her with the leaves. Oh well. I was glad to be the one to help. Mrs. Devers gave me another old sweater to keep me warm and we started to bag the leaves. It was hard to put them in bags because they would slip out the side and fall to the ground. When we tried to compact them, they would just fluff up again. This was harder than I thought. We worked for a while and finally finished.

"Thank you, child. May I give you a cup of cocoa before you head on home?"

"Sure," I said. So we went into her cozy, warm kitchen and she heated up the water.

I said, "You know, I didn't realize how hard it was to rake and bag the leaves. I just always thought of them as fun to step on and look at."

She looked at me with a far off look trying to remember her childhood. She said she used to do the same, but that is not how life is. We go through changes in our lives. Sometimes we stand out like the beauty of one single dandelion. Other times, we blend in with the crowd. Sometimes we slip off to the side to ponder our lives. But we are all part of the whole, so we have to do our job and pick up after ourselves. Her front yard did look nice and neat after we finished our work on the leaves.

I sipped the cocoa and listened to her voice. She was lonely. Her husband died years ago and her kids only came to see her on the weekends. I asked her if she would mind if I helped her rake and bag the leaves in the backyard.

"No," she said. "That would be wonderful. I would appreciate the help."

As I left, I waved and walked home. I forgot to return the sweater. Oh well, I could take it over tomorrow.

As I walked into my home with my cheeks all red and my eyes bright, my mother took me into her arms and kissed the top of my head. "Welcome home, my lovely daughter. Thank you for helping Mrs. Devers with her work."

I looked at her and smiled and thanked her for her love.

My mom asked, "Were you warm enough?"

"Yes," I said, "When I am helping another person, then I don't think of myself. I was warmed by Mrs. Devers' sweater and the smile on her face as we worked and talked. It was wonderful, Mom. I learned about life while looking at those leaves and listening to Mrs. Devers. I learned a lot from just looking around me."

27 | HELLO

Madeline was late for work, as usual. She ran up the sidewalk, past the bagel stand and into her building. She was hungry, but that would have to wait. She rushed over to the elevator and pushed the button marked "up." While she waited, a nice-looking man walked up beside her. He smiled and she smiled back, but then she kept her eyes glued to the door.

"Come on," she said. "Hurry up, elevator. I am late."

The man said, "Good morning."

She said, "Hello."

He asked how she was.

She replied, "OK."

He was looking at her and she was feeling uncomfortable. What did he want? Maybe she shouldn't get on the same elevator with him? She wished there were other people around. She tapped her foot. Where was that elevator? She was late.

The man asked if she was late. She finally smiled and said, "Well, I guess that is apparent since I am tapping my foot." He laughed a deep, hearty laugh and said that she had no choice but to wait, so she might as well relax. He introduced himself and said that he was starting a new business and had just leased a new space. He told her that he was looking for some help and asked if she knew of anyone. She was interested and inquired about the position and the qualifications.

She realized that she was qualified for the job. She had been praying just last night to find a new job that would be challenging and that she would enjoy. She looked at him again, with more interest this time.

She said, "I might be interested. What is your suite number and when can we set up an employment interview?"

He said they were already talking, and asked if he could just have a resume. She said, "Of course. I will drop it off on my break."

The elevator came and they both got on. She got off first and said goodbye. As she walked to her desk, she had a smile on her face. Everyone noticed this and wondered what had happened. She never had a smile on her face. In fact, she hardly even said hello to them. How unusual. She usually just ran by and paid no attention to anyone.

During her break, she stopped by the gentleman's office and dropped off her resume. She looked around and knew that this job was what she was looking for. She smiled at him, waved and left the office. She then went down to get a bagel and smiled at the person next to her and said hi. She was really happy for a change and wanted to spread her happiness around. The person next to her did not return her smile or her greeting. She just frowned and looked ahead. How rude, she wondered to herself. Doesn't she see that it is nice to be friendly? Then she thought of the way she normally was and sighed. She was like that, too. Maybe it was time to change. If she was nice, if she smiled and said hello, then other people might be in a better mood also. She would try this new way of life and see how it worked.

All day during work she was happy and those around her were happy. She got on the elevator and greeted everyone with a smile and a kind remark.

She went to the grocery store and smiled at the checkout person and said his name. "Hi Mike, how are you today? Isn't it a great day?"

Mike jerked his head up in surprise. How nice that she noticed him. Most people didn't say anything unless the grocery price was too high.

She whistled as she drove home and greeted her husband and child with a friendly smile and hug. "What a nice day," she said.

Her family was surprised and responded in kind. "Why was it such a good day?"

"Oh," she said, "I met a nice gentleman on the elevator and he might have a new job for me."

Her husband said that she had received a phone call from the gentleman who she mentioned. She called him back and they made an agreement for her to start her new job in two weeks at a much higher salary that she was making now. All these good things happened because a stranger had been nice enough to say hello to her.

That night she got down on her knees and thanked her heavenly Father for answering her prayers. But she also thanked him for a great lesson in optimism and kindness. She had not recognized how narrow her field of vision was and how much her manner and lack of warmth affected those around her. She vowed to smile and say hello as often as she could. Maybe she could start an epidemic of smiling.

Thank you, Heavenly Father. She needed to learn that lesson, and so do all of us as well.

28 | DO I HAVE A PURPOSE?

There was a little lamb who baa'd and baa'd and suckled her mother's milk. She pranced around and baa'd all day long. One day her mother noticed that she was awfully quiet. Why wasn't she prancing around and making little lamb noises. Was she okay?

The little lamb looked at her mother with soft eyes and said, "Is that all there is to my life, Mom? I get my love and food from you and I prance around and say 'baa.' Do I have a purpose here?"

Her mother looked at her with loving eyes and said, "My lovely daughter, you were born with a purpose. You are beauty and perfection. You are love and joy to behold. I am here to sustain and nurture you until you are old enough to do this for others. When you grow up you will wear a skin of much value. Your wool will be gently sheared from your back and it will be woven into cloth to keep people warm. You have a GREAT purpose for your life."

The lamb looked in awe at her mother. "But what of the other lambs?" she asked. "Do they all serve a purpose?"

"Of course," her mother said, "We all have our work to do. We all have a purpose. Why else would we be born?"

5 JOURNEYS

29 | THE BEGINNING

How do you describe the beginning of everything?
Some start with science.
You search and dig,
You name and exclaim!
You read and study to find out how it happened.
In the process, you expand your mind and feed your knowledge.
You experiment and extrapolate;
You invent wonderful items to ease the world.
You create cloth and clothing.
You utilize wood for houses.
You invent sources of light and harness energy to heat and cool your lives.
You sing songs and dance waltzes.
You run on air and fly through the skies.
You leap across boundaries that do not exist because of your vision of new
    concepts.
You delve deeper and look at the movement of the universe.
You circle the planets and look under the oceans.
You grow food and feed millions.
You invent microwaves, cyberspace, computers and more.
Your creativity, together with knowledge, is endless and exciting.

Isn't this fun? What is next? Who knows?

But where did all this start and how does it continue?
What is the meaning of all this activity?

What about God?
God created you as a spirit and molded your body.
Jesus sustains and forgives you when you repent and improve.
Do you believe this?
Who creates? You, or a combination of you and God?
Who performs miraculous feats un-envisioned before?
Who puts the ideas in your head?
Are you creating alone or with the assistance of the Holy Spirit?

What is the beginning and what is eternity? Aren't both enigmas the same?
Who put in place all you see and all that you are?

Can everyone partake of this creative process?
When you do, are you fulfilled?
Are you satisfied with what you have achieved? Aren't you great!

Of course you are. You come from the lineage of God. How else could you feel?
Is there really a mystery here? No, not really.
Can you accept that you can become part of a higher order of life? Why not?

How does your creative process work? Do you do it in partnership with God?

Remember your beginning with your Heavenly Father and know the Answer.

30 | THE PIE OF LIFE

There once was a pie that was made of all the best ingredients. It was pecan and apple, persimmon and perseverance, perspective and focus. It was filled with raisins and cinnamon, common sense and creativity. It was encased in love and filled with reason and righteousness. It was filled with the ingredients from God and eaten by many.

Some eat to fill their bellies, others eat to improve. Some just smell the aroma but forget to taste its sweetness. Some look with longing but do not venture close enough to eat.

Eat of the pie of life and fill your moment with sweetness and expectation. Fill your spirit with God's love and share your piece of life with your fellow human beings. Each piece is filled with a variety of spices and experiences. Each piece is cut differently but re-forms into perfect harmony. Each piece is part of the whole and can realign with perfect precision.

The dough of life is kneaded and needed. When it is pushed and rolled out, it is used to enclose the top and bottom layers of the pie. It becomes the shell of existence and the circle of life's connection.

God is the foundation. God is the whole pie and all the pieces. Each piece is made from the same ingredients, but filled with the spice of human life. Each piece has the mark of experiences and expectations. Each piece fits together as it is refined and realigns with God's spirit. Each piece, once eaten and digested, becomes part of and then one with the pie of life.

31 | THE CLAY OF EXISTENCE

There was a maker of pots. All day long he molded the clay and spun the wheel of fortune. His hands molded the clay into objects of everyday use. His hands created the structure while the wheel turned and a shape emerged. At each turn, he could decide to place just a little more pressure and change the entire use of the pot. It was in his whim to make the pot tall or slim, fat or stocky—a thing of fragile beauty or a thick stock pot. He had the ability to shape, form, mold and design the pot of life.

He could drink from it, eat from it, hold objects in it or just look at it. He could put it into the fire and burnish it with color and texture. It was all up to him. One touch of a hand or one breath and all could change. Too much fire or too little time could shatter the pot into shards or chip away at its exterior.

Each human is molded from the clay of existence.
Each pot is filled with desires, love, and expectations.
Each pot is filled with the gifts of the Holy Spirit.
Each pot is filled with talents, hopes and desires.
Each pot can be filled to overflowing with love for family and others.
Each pot is molded from the same clay of life.

Don't let others chip away and destroy it.
Contribute what is good to your clay of existence
Fill your pot with the best there is and share it with others.

32 | THE NEIGHBORS

She was standing in the kitchen talking to the repairman who was working on her refrigerator.

She said, "I am so used to all of these modern conveniences. I don't know how to get along without them. I had the hot water heater replaced last week. The week before was the air conditioner and the sprinkler system. Then to top it all off, the electricity went off for an entire day. I was absolutely lost. I did not have any candles or even a flashlight. I am not very mechanical and I live here alone. My children called to make sure I was all right. At least the phone worked. Without the phone, I would not have had any communication at all. I was going to get in my car and go to my children's home, but I did not have enough gas. I thought to myself, I wonder if the gas stations are working. I believe the pumps use electricity. I couldn't turn on the television. I couldn't cook. I couldn't even read after it was dark.

"I suddenly remembered my neighbor. She had to use an oxygen pump to stay alive. I ran over to her house and banged on the door and called to her. 'Are you all right in there? Edna, are you OK?' I did not hear anyone. I ran around the house trying to look in the windows. I saw Edna sitting in a chair waving to me. She was all right. She had purchased a battery operated unit but it would not last long. I called her children and they came over and took her home with them. Well, at least one crisis was over.

"Boy, I thought, we sure depend on electricity for everything. I don't know how I could survive without it. I looked around for something to do. The house was so quiet. Normally I had the television running all the time. It kept me company. I didn't know my other neighbors or even the ones across the street. I decided that I would go outside. The house was getting awfully warm.

"I noticed that many people were outside. They had pulled out some chairs and were sitting on their front lawns. They were all talking together so I went over and joined them. We introduced ourselves and started to tell about our lives. Each one listened and interacted. It was wonderful. We all went into our homes and brought out fruit and food so it wouldn't spoil. We shared our food and our thoughts. This is what a neighborhood should be like. We really have nice neighbors. We had a lot in common.

"When it got dark, we all went inside and said how we would get together again, real soon. We all had a great time getting to know one another. When I returned to the house, the lights flickered on and the power was restored. The television came on and so did the air conditioner. But I noticed that the refrigerator never did come on again, so I called you to come help me."

The repairman asked, "Did you and your neighbors ever get together again?"

"You know, we haven't yet but we will. I hope we will."

33 | A SIDE OF FRIES

There was a waitress who chewed gum with a crackle. She talked and slapped people on the back. You could hear her voice ring out to the chef with her order for breakfast, lunch or dinner.

"Two fried eggs and hash browns," she exclaimed as she chewed her gum. Snap went the gum as she sauntered between tables. "Two BLTs and one club sandwich to go. Two grilled cheese sandwiches and a side of fries. One milkshake and a piece of apple pie."

She had a wide grin and everyone loved her. She chewed and chewed that gum and called everyone "Honey." She was called Sally. Yep, Sally was her name. She wore a paisley dress and a white apron around her waist. She kept unruly kids in their seats and took no nonsense from any of the customers. They all loved her. They went to the diner just to hear the comfort of her voice. "Two boiled eggs and some milk. Two sides of ham and make it quick!"

One day in mid-sentence she stopped and let her tray fall to the floor. She clutched her chest and fell. Someone yelled and called for help; another grabbed her so she wouldn't hit her head on the floor; another started CPR while they all stayed until help arrived. They rushed her to a hospital and all waited for the doctor's reply.

She would be fine, but it would take a while. Flowers poured in, along with gifts and cards. People felt her loss at the diner and sauntered over to visit. Many brought her food and others helped pay her bills. Many just tried to find a new place to eat, but it wasn't the same. Sally was important in their lives, and they needed to do something for her in return. They visited and tried to comfort and help her laugh. They cared and loved her.

Sally was amazed. She had raised a passel of kids: some of her own plus a few who would walk in and out of her house. She was overly generous and took life as it came. She knew right from wrong and never diverted from the right path. Her kids wanted her to stay with them, but Sally said, "No. I know you love me and care, but my life is here. Let me be for now. Just come see me as often as you can."

Soon Sally gained her strength and was able to return to the diner. The day she arrived was a great celebration. Her friends sat her down and waited on her. All, of course, chewed gum and snapped it with acclaim.

"Hi, Honey," they said. "What do you want today?" Sally looked at them and let out a great laugh.

"Did I look like that, chewing and snapping gum and calling everyone 'Honey'?"

"Yes," they said. "We love you and love the way you do it. You are so real. There is no pretense or pretending. We always came here because of you—certainly not the food."

Sally was overwhelmed—All of this love because she was someone that didn't pretend. She was amazed. How else should people live their lives?

34 | THE MENDED FENCE

John and Cindy had been married for twenty years. They had two teenagers and an eight-year-old girl. They lived in a moderate home with three bedrooms and two and one-half baths. John worked as a salesman and Cindy was a school teacher.

Every weekend, Cindy had a list of jobs that needed to be done. "Mend the fence" was always first on the list. She also had things like wash the windows, clean out the garage, fix the bike, wash the car, do laundry, grocery shopping, etc. Each week, Cindy dispensed the jobs to everyone in the house and expected the work to be done. She always gave John the slip that said "mend the fence." Every week he tried to find the time to go to the store and buy the wood and nails to fix the fence, but he never completed his assigned task.

The dog got loose because there was a gap in the fence, so they had to chase him every day. The hole got larger and larger, but John never found the time to mend the fence. Cindy nagged and John just became obstinate. "The hole is not that big. It can be patched. I will take care of it."

Then one day, a stray cat crawled through the fence and went after their dog. The dog chased the cat and their little girl started yelling and then crying. The cat ran into the house with the dog close behind. The chase was on and nothing was excluded from their path. *Crash* went the lamp. Down went the china vase from Aunt Louise. The cat jumped on to the kitchen counter and ran through the food, then huddled on top of the refrigerator and snarled.

John chased the dog, caught him and threw him outside.

"Come here, little kitty. I won't hurt you."

The cat snapped at John and clawed his arm.

"Ouch," said John as he reached again for the cat. He grabbed the cat by the back of the neck and held it at arm's length. He ran to the front door and threw the cat out.

He ran into the garage and found a scrap piece of wood and some nails and covered that hole in the fence.

"There," he said. "That will keep you out!"

He went inside and carefully washed and sanitized his wound.

Just then, Cindy came home from shopping and looked at the mess. Her favorite vase was broken and her face became red.

"What happened?" she asked.

John looked up from bandaging his arm. With a sheepish grin, he said, "Well, I finally mended the fence."

Apologies can be difficult, so do not procrastinate and do what is necessary to get your lives in order.

35 | LATER

There was a perky girl whose smile lit up her face and deepened the dimples in her plump cheeks. She always wore a blue ribbon in her hair to match the color of her eyes. She was all girl and refused to wear pants at all. In fact, she insisted on her way about everything. When she was angry, her ribbon would droop and her lip would quiver. She stomped her foot and wrapped her dad around her little finger. "Do this!" she demanded, and her father gave in. It was easier to give in than say no!

Her mother looked on with sadness in her heart, for she knew that her daughter was on the wrong path. If she had no respect for her parent's decisions, would she try to control all her friends and acquaintances the same way? Would she come to know the difference between right and wrong?

The mom gently took her daughter to her room to talk with her. Did her daughter understand the difference between love and kindness and manipulation and control?

Her daughter's eyes became dark and her cheeks flushed red. Of course she understood! Her daddy always gave her everything because he loved her.

Her mother tried to help her understand the difference by pointing out that she had a tantrum before her dad agreed. Did she understand the difference between asking and demanding?

The little girl went over to her closet and opened the door. She said, "Look, Mom. Look at all the pretty dresses I have and the shoes to match. I am so pretty and feminine. My daddy just wants to do what I ask of him."

Her mother sighed and said, "Daughter, you are so very lovely, but looks and tears do not always get you what you want. It is important to think through your choices carefully. Many times you should not get what you ask for."

Her daughter looked at her with wonder and a total disregard for her words. She had everything she wanted and she always wanted it immediately and got it.

Her mother sighed and stroked her daughter's hair. She knew that her daughter's future rested in her own hands. Her daughter needed to change the course of her selfishness. She would have to talk with her husband later.

She saw a vision of her child's willfulness getting worse as she controlled everyone and everything around her. She saw her child alone and without friends. She saw her overachieve and strive for fame and fortune. She saw her become a success with money and adoration.

She saw her walking down a lonely path, seeking a way to fill the emptiness inside. She saw her drinking alcohol and taking drugs to be accepted by others. She saw her child marry several men and have children with abandon. She looked deep into her child's eyes and knew that she and her husband must take responsibility and warn her of the problems that lay ahead if she continued on this path.

She walked out of her daughter's bedroom and quietly shut the door. The vision she saw startled her, for she knew it was true.

She walked into the living room and turned to her husband to talk. He was snoring in front of the television. The lines on his face were relaxed. She would talk with him later and they would change the way they were raising their daughter.

Later. They would talk later.

36 | ONE STEP AT A TIME

There are people who wish for life to change. They look out their windows and wish upon a star. But nothing changes and they are disappointed again.

There was a woman who had great burdens. She lacked schooling, even though she had been given the opportunity to attend. She thought school was a waste of time so she quit after the ninth grade. She had many children, who ranged in age from a few weeks to six-years-old, and no husband. But she was bored. She wanted more than to sit in the apartment and tend her children. Something had to change.

She did not need to get an education and earn a living since the checks always arrived, monthly, from the government. She could eat, sleep and watch television. But one day, as she sat bored in her room, she decided she wanted something better. She wanted to change. She did not like this existence. It wasn't right. But what could she do? She had to watch her kids.

She bundled all the kids up and went outside. The air was fresh, but all around her was clutter and dirt. The streets were filled with debris and there was garbage everywhere. Her apartment and the outside of the building looked the same. Someone ought to clean this mess up, she thought. Wait a minute, she thought, I guess the apartment is my responsibility and I don't even do that. But I don't really have the time or the materials to keep it clean. She had some money in her pocket and wondered what she should spend it on. She had enough food. Maybe she could get a coke. She sauntered into the grocery store. She decided to clean up her act so she bought some soap and other cleaning supplies. That afternoon, she went home and scrubbed her apartment. This was better. I will take it one step at a time. She bathed her children and they smelled clean. How nice, she thought. Then she cleaned up herself and felt so much better.

Someone knocked at her door. She opened it up to see the social worker. She normally hated her visit, but today was glad to see her.

The worker came in and her mouth opened wide.

"This place looks great! What changed?" she asked.

The girl said that she was tired of her life and the garbage place it had become. She wanted to change. So she took the first step. The social worker asked her if she was serious.

"Yes," she said.

"Then let's put the kids in daycare and I will get you trained for a job. You will need to finish your education and study to become something other than what you presently are."

"Okay," the girl said. "Let's go for it."

Together they planned out her new life. It became obvious to the girl that much effort and time, much study and organization would be needed. But she still wanted to take one step at a time, so the first year she studied and got her GED. She started to train as a secretary and got a job. She made enough money to move into a better place. Her kids were learning, also. She became stricter and made sure they wore clean clothes and toed the line. She kept studying and then went on to college. She studied some more and became a nurse. Her kids were in school and made her proud. She wanted them to know that they had to work for what they received.

Then one day, she went back to the old neighborhood and the old apartments. They were still dirty and garbage was still outside the door. She walked by one of the apartments and saw a young girl surrounded by babies.

She softly knocked on the door and said, "May I come in and talk to you?"

"Sure," said the girl, "but I don't think I will listen to you."

The girl walked into the little, dirty room and said, "Let's just talk about taking one step at a time."

37 | THE ROSE

There was a late bloomer whose beauty was like a perfect rose. Her hair was a dusty red and her eyes silver green. She had long legs and a perfect smile. She was shy. She went to college and decided to be a doctor. She felt a kinship to others and felt complete only when she helped those less fortunate. She knew that she would have to work really hard and study so she could get into medical school. She made it and then went on to specialize in elderly care.

Her patients loved her, for she had a kind and loving demeanor. She wore the scent of rose petals and everyone she saw remembered the times in their lives they received lovely rose flowers. They remembered birthdays and anniversaries. They remembered when their kids showed up with a single rose on Mother's Day with a handmade card. They remembered the roses growing along the trellis behind their house. Her patients remembered, and it blotted out the pain of the doctor's treatments.

Somehow it was easier to continue on with the treatments when their precious doctor was around. She would come into their room and take hold of their hands.

"How are you today?" she would say with compassion and caring in her voice. "Is there anything that I can do to help you?"

One of her patients said, "Yes, will you pray with me?"

The doctor knew that her patient's time was near. She said, "Of course." Calm and peace filled them both as they prayed.

How nice, she thought. There is more I can do for my patients beyond the medicine and surgery. How nice to know there is another way to help people.

The older patient sighed and said, "Thank you. I can rest now."

As she watched, her patient slipped away and took her last breath. The room filled with light and the scent of roses remained. The doctor knew that her work was complete. She sought the help of her healing profession, but she also sought the healing from her Heavenly Father.

She got up from her chair with tears in her eyes. She thanked her Heavenly Father for giving her the words and knowledge to help others, for the blossoming of a human's spirit is nurtured with love and caring.

The doctor walked out of the room, but looked back for just a second. Her patient lay sleeping for eternity.

38 | THE ONE THAT GOT AWAY

Larry was ten years old. His dad promised him that they would go fishing in the morning. He was so excited. They had already gone to the store and bought a fishing rod, reel and colored lures. He had his own tackle box and a bright orange hat for his head.

He put out his clothes that night so he could slip them on quickly first thing in the morning. Soon, he heard his dad come in.

"Wake up, son. It is time to go fishing."

He got up and put on his clothes in two minutes flat. He was ready. They packed up the car and took the picnic basket his mom gave them. Off they went.

The sun was just coming up. His father explained that they needed to catch the fish early in the morning when the fish were hungry.

Just over the hill, Larry saw the lake.

"Wow! This is neat, Dad."

They quietly got out of the car and took their gear. Larry had his pole and reel, his tackle box and orange hat. He was ready. They walked to the lake and Larry's dad fixed his fishing pole and attached the line and lure. Then he showed him how to cast it out into the water. *Whirr* went the reel as the line fed out. He practiced and after a while got the hang of it. He cast and cast. Every time he reeled in, he saw his lure glitter in the sun. He watched the fish chase the lure, but they never caught up to it. Maybe he should reel it in slower so they could swim fast enough to catch the lure. He tried and tried but couldn't seem to match the lure with the fish. Oh well, this was fun being with his dad.

After a while, they rested on a blanket and Larry's dad gave him homemade biscuits and orange juice. They both lay down and took a nap.

Suddenly, Larry woke up. He thought he heard something. His dad was snoring next to him. He looked out at the lake and saw a fish move the water. How neat. So he got up and cast his lure far out into the lake. He knew it was perfect. Out the lure flew, as if it knew just where to land on the water. Larry let it sink down just a little before he started to reel it in. Soon, he felt a sharp tug and he knew that he had a fish on his line. So he pulled and tugged. The fish was strong and kept on fighting, but Larry knew he was stronger, so he kept on reeling it in. Then he caught sight of the fish. It was long and slender and had whiskers like a cat.

"Wow," he said. "This must be a catfish."

He had eaten one at a restaurant just last week. He didn't realize the fish really looked like a cat. He stood there at the edge wondering what to do. He hated to wake up his dad, but he could not stand there all day looking at the fish swimming back and forth. So he just sat down and waited. Pretty soon, his dad woke up and looked for his son. He returned to the lake and saw the fish on the line.

"Son, do you want to keep him or throw him back?"

The son thought for a while. "If I keep him, can I put him in the bathtub at home?"

"No, Son, we will clean and eat him for dinner."

"If I throw him back, will he be here next time for me to catch again?"

"Possibly," said the dad.

"You decide for me, Dad."

"No," said the father. "This is your choice. Keep him on the line or let him go."

"Well," said the son, "I will let him go."

So the dad released the fish and packed up their gear to go home.

Larry said, "Dad, is fishing like life?"

"What do you mean, Son?"

"You know, Dad, when Mark and I were friends, Mark wanted to tell me what to do. He would boss me around like a fish on a line. But after I told him I didn't want to be friends anymore, then I felt free. Do you think the fish feels the same way?"

Larry's dad looked at his wise son and said, "I am sure he does, Son. I am sure he does."

Each of us is free to make our own choices in life. We should choose wisely.

39 | THE VISION

Once upon a time, in a land that existed a long time ago, there lived a princess of great beauty and warmth. She was renowned for her grace and kindness. The prince was, of course, charming and very handsome. After a royal wedding, they had ten children and their lands prospered, as well as all the people living there. The children grew up and multiplied and spread across the face of the land both near and far. Each one married and had children. Pretty soon, the world expanded and great rivers were crossed and new lands inhabited. New countries were formed and great families arose. But everyone was related to the original princely couple.

Every once in a while the princess would hear from her far-off children asking for advice. But she also heard of wars and battles where people died. She heard of great burnings and also great prosperity. She heard of worlds unknown and family gatherings to which she was invited. She listened to their mistakes, shared their happiness, gloried in their triumphs, and wept with them as well.

One lovely morning she was sitting in her room wondering why there was so much death and destruction. Why would countries declare war on each other? After all, they were all brothers and sisters. Why should they hurt one another? She shook her head and a tear spilled down her cheek. What could have turned brother against brother? We are all from the same family. Why would they harm one another?

She walked into her husband's study. The light was streaming in the window and his grey hair shone. She touched his head and soothed his cheek. "My husband, my love, I do not understand? Please give me some of your time and explain to me what happened. I had a great vision for our children to live in peace and contentment. They multiplied and spread across this great world. They wandered near and far and created other children and other ways. My vision for peace has fallen apart. They are all our children. How could they not understand that when they do wrong to each other, they are killing their own family?"

Her princely husband looked at her with sad eyes. "Yes, my lovely wife, I know of your vision. I share it as well. When we found each other, I prayed to God for his vision and the peace and love that has prospered our people and our lives. I asked for God's love to permeate everything that we do and every family member. God agreed and revealed his laws and his plan of salvation to guide us. We should live according to the laws God gave us and the salvation of Jesus Christ. The vision was passed down from generation to generation, but God also gave us agency to choose for ourselves. His vision was for us all to choose him and to follow his plan. So why would we not do that? God has provided so much for us and we could live in peace and the shelter of his love. What joy we have on this earth.

"Some of our children chose another way. They chose a path of lies, greed, power over others, deceit and dishonesty. They sought the world and its silver and gold. They did not understand that all that we have is because of God's blessings. They could have had everything if they had chosen the right things in their lives. Instead, they chose a different path that was strewn with waste and death. It was piled up with bodies and things. They climbed a large hill only to fall by the wayside.

"So many of our children sought the wrong path, but we cannot choose for them nor force them. We can only be an example for them based on our vision. That is all we can do and pray that they return."

Neither will God force us to do good, only invite us to do so. However, we are all of the same princely family, so why would we want to harm each other? Isn't there a better way, a better vision?

6 THE SYMPHONY OF LIFE

40 | EMERGENCE

In the silence of the moment, I hear God's quiet voice. He whispers in my mind the glory of his world.

Behold the vistas of the mountains.
Behold the everlasting light.
Behold the grandeur of the Rockies.
Behold the land of greening grass and tides of night.
Behold the moments of reflection as the quiet fills with song.
Behold a mind whose thoughts extend beyond the world we see.
Behold the substance of love as thick and liquid as a field of gold.
Behold the smell of sweet beginnings through the waters of life.
Behold the strength of faith through the courage of our Lord.
Behold the invitation of desire as your spirit yearns for food.
Behold the fulfillment of your substance through the redemption of
    Christ.
Behold the meaning of all there is through the eternity of truth.

41 | CHORUS OF ANGELS

Join the Chorus of Angels as they sing God's praises.

There was a girl with a voice like an angel. She sang in churches on Sundays with such great feeling that everyone held their breath. Tears would form in their eyes as they remembered their deepest memories. Some thought of their dearly departed. Some thought of their children. Some thought of times long past. Some thought of their feelings for God.

The girl that sang thought only of God and tried each Sunday to get her message across. One day, a talent agent sat in the church and heard her sing. He was astounded at the depth of her feeling. He went up to her after church and asked if she would consider singing in his national choir. She inquired further. She listened and sought the wisdom of her Heavenly Father before she made a decision. She felt it was right and agreed to join the group. Quickly, she started to sing the lead and everyone was amazed at her talent. The choir changed from mere singers to a true choir of angels as they poured out their hearts to all who would hear.

During practice one day, everyone gathered round to find out her secret. She simply said she loved God and wanted everyone to know.

"But why?" they asked. "How can you be so certain?"

She said, "How can you not be certain? Why, he is everywhere. He is your love. He is your feeling. He is your creativity. He watches over us. He sent his son to forgive us of repented sins and save our lives. How could you not be grateful? Would you send your own son out to die for the whole world? Would your son take the responsibility for saving my life and all others? Would he forgive you and still love you? When you seek his advice does he always tell you the truth? Can you trust him completely? Can you compare anyone on earth to this man of God called Jesus Christ?"

They sat there a moment in silence. "We never thought of him that way before."

She said, "Why don't you try?"

That night the choir sang like never before. They sang their praises to God for their blessings. They thanked him for their lives. They sang out their love to him. The audience was in tears. They heard the emotion and felt the love. How incredible. They all went home and loved their families and friends more. Their lives were better because of their wonderful songs to God.

Soon, news of the choir reached others and the choir was booked to sing all over the world. The more their love reached out the more they prospered.

Then one day, the girl disappeared. The choir was desperate to find her. Where had she gone?

A letter was delivered before the show.

>   My Dearest Friends,
>   I leave you now to seek new people so they can also feel God's love, if they choose. You are on the right path. Do not forget who you are.
>   Love,
>   Your Angel

42 | EVERYONE TOGETHER

The conductor started to wave his baton. The members of the orchestra were alert and ready to give the performance of their lives. The choir had voices like angels. The entire evening would be one to remember. Each section of the orchestra was important. Every voice and every instrument fit together to form a perfect sound. The leader's responsibilities were vast. He had to remember what each instrument and each voice did so that everyone worked together.

The audience sat in their chairs. When the music started, each person sat up straight and leaned closer to the sounds that were coming to them from the stage. How could this perfect tone be delivered from such a variety of instruments, voices and talents? What was this miracle of togetherness that they all felt? Everything worked together in unison. The experience was total. Everyone participated: the orchestra, the choir and the audience.

When the sound stopped, the audience rose to their feet and clapped until their hands hurt. "Bravo," they yelled. "Bravo." The people on the stage bowed and saluted their audience. The audience clapped and thanked the musicians and choir for a job well done.

They all worked together that night to harmonize and enjoy the wonder of the evening. The conductor faced the audience and bowed to them. He had orchestrated the entire event. He conducted a few moments of their lives tonight and was grateful it all worked together. What a wonderful evening.

Consider how God has given us talents so that we can work together, with him, in perfect harmony.

43 | THE ANGELIC CHOIR

There is a symphony of life that hasn't been heard in decades.
This music is the lyric song of God.
The choir is of angelic voices and the words are of cherishing and love.
The efforts of God upon the earth can orchestrate you towards immortal life,
if you will pick up a lyric of joy.

Feel the strings of the harp vibrate with life.
Hear the sound of the drums as they beat out the evil.
Feel the vibration of the reeds as the breath of life renews each child that is
born.
Feel the sounds of the bow moving across the strings of time.
Feel the eternal sounds of voices lifted up in prayer.
Feel your spiritual power growing, and live again within the symphony of
God.

44 | THE SONG

Love fuels the soul.
Love is truly a substance to be reckoned with.
Through love and caring, anything can be accomplished.

Try and think of a time upon the earth when everyone was at peace.
Try and remember when everyone on the earth thought of the next person
    first.
Try and remember when everyone on the earth smiled in the space of a day.
Try and remember when everyone on earth worshiped their one and only true
    God.
Try and remember what the earth was like when everyone knew they were
    God's children.
Try and remember when everyone recognized that Jesus Christ was their
    Savior and redeemer of their souls.
Try and remember where you began and what eternity means.
Try and remember the spiritual essence of yourselves as you work and live
    each moment of the day.
Try and remember to love each other as God loves you.
Try and remember that God and Jesus Christ are as real as you are.
Try and remember to look deeply into your lives and separate out the good
    from the evil and the love from the hate.
Try and grab hold of the precious moments of your lives.

Join together all the people of the earth
    and sing the praises of God, our Father, through his son, Jesus Christ.
Sing together in unison.
Sing the love songs of God.
Sing the songs of Faith and Glory.
Sing, O Sing along.

45 | PARTAKING

There was a world covered with snow. Each flake was piled upon each other to form a mound. It increased in volume and formed a huge snow bank.

The little boy ventured out into the hushed dawn. The world was quiet, for the snow muffled the sounds. *Crunch* was the sound as he walked onward. He was the first one out into the wonderland of white and his steps the first ones made in the new snow.

He saw a lonely cardinal on a pine branch. He just watched and saw the contrast of the red against white in the early rising of the day.

He was dressed warmly in his high-topped boots and parka made from goose down. He smelled the clean air and thanked God for a perfect day. As he ventured out he noticed that everything was white. So much snow had fallen that even the cars could not be seen. He could see his breath puff out as he walked. He made patterns in the snow. He walked in circles and back and forth. He made snow angels and started working on a snowman. What fun.

Pretty soon he heard a voice calling. "Son! Oh, Son! Breakfast is ready. Come eat and warm up by the fire."

The boy turned around and, with glowing eyes and red cheeks, yelled, "I will be right there, Mom." His mom smiled as she saw her small boy bundled in his warm clothes prancing around in the snow. Soon he came in and she unpeeled the layers of clothing and found her laughing boy beneath.

"Did you have a good time, Son? Did you see the wonders of God early this morning?"

"Yes, Mother, I did."

He hugged his mom and snuggled in her embrace. The love they felt for each other was overwhelming. The moment was perfect and the praise to God complete.

As they sat down to eat they were joined by the rest of the family. Looks like another beautiful day.

Thank you, Lord, for all your love and beauty.
Thank you for the abundance you place before us.
Thank you for your son, Jesus Christ.
Thank you for our lives.
Thank you for this day.

46 | What Time Is It?

"What time is it?" I asked.

"It is 4:45 and almost time to leave work," they replied.

Oh great. I had ten phone calls yet and something to get into overnight mail. I asked, "Would you help me finish this project?"

My co-worker replied, "I would like to help, but I need to leave now. I will next time."

So I just continued to work until the job was done. This seemed to happen every night. I wondered why all the other workers were able to leave exactly at 5:00. It didn't seem right.

Finally, I finished my work, got in my car and started for home. I looked at the sky. It was beautiful, for the sun was just setting. I decided to exit the highway and stopped my car on a vacant lot to get a better view.

Oh, this is so nice, I thought. I am glad that I left the office late so that I could watch this beautiful sunset. If I were home, I would just be watching television and listening to the news. This is much better.

Suddenly, it seemed as if I was watching more than a sunset. The sky turned a bright pink and then seemed to part in the middle. The sky opened up and a light of great intensity poured out of the opening. The rift became wider and wider and the light grew in magnitude. I was mesmerized. I felt great awe. I got out of my car and stared at the sky. Quiet surrounded me. The light enveloped everything in its path: the trees, buildings, cars, homes, the people and then me. I was surrounded by this incredible light. I started to cry, for I had never felt such love and happiness. What was happening?

I closed my eyes and enjoyed the great and wondrous feeling of love washing over and through me. It was a light of warmth and radiance that had no end and no beginning. It cleansed everything and everybody. I felt so clean and pure. I felt changed. I wanted to shout for joy.

I opened my eyes and the light seemed to be condensing and pulling back. It had a will of its own. It was pulled into the sky and became smaller and smaller. Soon it disappeared and all I saw was the setting sun. I blinked and blinked again. Did that really happen? I looked at the street in front of me where cars were streaming by at high velocities. People just kept on going at their fast pace, ignoring their surroundings. They had not even stopped or noticed. They were not standing next to their cars with wondrous expressions on their faces. In fact, I couldn't see their faces. They were a blur.

I saw a man quickly walk toward me. He was a nice looking man with a smile that lit up his face.

"Did you see that?" he asked. "Did you see that light? Did you feel the love? It was incredible."

I looked at him and said, "Yes! Oh, yes, I did. Tell me what you saw and felt."

So he did and I did and we talked and talked.

Soon, it was dark so we went to dinner and talked some more.

"How many people saw it, do you think?" I asked him.

"I don't know," he said, but explained how he noticed that cars were streaming by while it happened. "Can you imagine missing that event?"

"No," I said, "but sometimes, we get so busy we don't even look up."

"What time is it?" I asked?

He replied, "It is a beautiful time. It is God's time."

47 | LOVE IS ETERNAL

I am the father of a child, small and meek. She was beautiful to behold with blond curly hair and bright, blue eyes. It was as if her bubbly personality was encased in a body too small to contain it.

She affected people as they peered into her eyes. They felt a sense of joy and of purpose to their lives. She did not do anything extraordinary, just smiled. The effect was as lightning that struck at your heart. The light filled you up and then exited to fill another person that might be near you.

It was on a Wednesday at 6:02 pm when life changed. Nothing was expected. It was just an ordinary day. But an earthquake struck, and the home and life I had vanished under tons of rubble.

I was on my way home and the shaking brought me to my knees. By the time I reached my home, there was nothing there but piles of rock. I frantically tore at the rocks trying to get to my wife and precious, blue-eyed daughter. Others heard my cries and came running. Hour after hour we worked together. Many came knowing and remembering the bright light they felt upon meeting my precious one. Days passed and no sounds could be heard, no motion detected. All I could feel was darkness, hopelessness and despair.

Finally, I sat there amidst the rubble and prayed like I never did before. "If she is alive, Heavenly Father, please direct a beam of sunlight toward the spot where we should dig."

As if on cue, the sun peeked out from a cloud and pierced through the sky down to a point in the rubble. But as I stepped toward it, I saw another beam of light coming up from the ground to meet the one from above--the two beams of light were connecting. As I stepped into the light, my despair vanished. Love poured into me from above and below. I was part of a great oneness that flowed inside of me and then to others. I knew then that my daughter's love was continuing to flow even after her death. There was a new life in her that would reach beyond this world and never end. She was still with me and would be for all eternity.

7 CHOICES

48 | FROZEN IN PRAYER

The weather was stormy and the icy particles licked the windshield as the wipers went back and forth. The sound was in cadence with the radio that was blaring rock music. The driver leaned forward and tried to see a few feet in front of his car but could not. His friend was singing along with the music and bouncing up and down.

"Hey man, this music is great isn't it?" His friend was high on drugs and had no understanding of the danger of their situation.

The driver turned off the radio and the passenger just kept singing and bouncing around until he noticed he had no accompaniment. "Hey man," he said. "Why'd you turn off the music?"

The driver said, "Look outside. It is solid ice. I must concentrate on driving and your music and singing are definitely a distraction."

The passenger became quiet as he tried to peer outside. "Wow," he said. "Look at all the ice."

Pretty soon the windshield wipers stopped, for the ice was so thick that the windshield was frozen solid. The driver pulled over to the side and stopped the car.

Well, now what? They would have to wait for help. The ice and snow piled up. The sound was muffled and no other cars passed by. He had taken a shortcut and no one knew where they were.

His passenger started to come down from his high and began to cry and blame his friend. "Why'd you drive this way? I feel lousy. We need to do something."

"What do you suggest?" the driver asked.

"Well, I don't really know, man, but I feel awful." He got sick and the stench in the car was terrible. The driver tried to open his door but it was frozen shut. He pushed his friend into the back seat.

"Try the door back there. If we stay here we will die."

The doors would not budge. They were trapped in ice.

The friend said, "You know, I remember when mastodons were trapped in the ice and years later they were discovered."

"Thanks a lot," said the driver. "That was comforting to hear."

The driver had run away from home a year ago and was drifting from one place and job to another. He had never called his mom. She always warned him about this and that, but he got tired of listening and so he left. He had better things to do with his life than to be controlled by her silly rules.

Well, he sure learned fast that a life without rules and direction can lead you to the shortcuts.

This shortcut was obviously the wrong one to take. He looked at his friend who was shivering and shaking. His lips were blue and icy particles had dried where tears had formed. The driver knew he looked the same. He also knew they would die.

As the driver reflected back on his life, he tried to think of the good things he did for his parents and others. Unfortunately, he could only remember a few instances. He regretted his choices to live this life without rules. Now it would end so soon, but what could he do? Maybe he could pray.

The car was discovered by a police officer the following week. When he pried open the door, he found two young boys.

The passenger was frozen with fear upon his face.

The driver was frozen in prayer.

The policeman shook his head. He was witnessing this more and more. He wished that these kids could learn to lead wholesome lives before it was too late. How sad that these lives had been cut short.

As the police lifted the kids out of the car, the sun came out and reflected on their icicle tears.

49 | HOW MANY?

God had a meeting in heaven long before the earth was created. We were his spirit children and were all invited to attend. He explained his plan of salvation to come to earth, gain our mortal bodies and return home again. We agreed and shouted for joy! So the process of creation of the earth began.

To succeed, this plan would require a Savior. There were two volunteers: Jesus Christ and Lucifer.

Lucifer said, "I have the best plan. I will guarantee that all your children will come back home, just leave it to me."

"What did you have in mind?" asked God.

"I will make sure they all return, for I will take from them their will so they will have no choice but to obey me and come back to you. By doing this, I will be in charge and I will get the credit for their return. I will be triumphant."

But God said, "I will not allow you to tamper with the wills of my children. They are my children, made in my image, and they will return to me of their own free will or not at all. I have already explained my plan and you will not do this. I have picked Jesus Christ to be their Savior and through him, he will redeem my children, if they repent and choose to follow him and his teachings on the earth."

Lucifer's face transformed to hate and a great battle ensued in heaven. Lucifer lost and, as a spirit, was cast out to the earth, along with a third of God's spirit children who chose to follow him. They would continue this battle on the earth and would make God and his other children pay with their very souls.

So Lucifer and his minions devised a plan to tempt Eve and bring their downfall. God's children began to arrive on the earth. Thus began the fight for our wills, our right to choose and remember our Father in Heaven. The temptations got worse and great fighting occurred in the land. Many people were killed, as they chose to side with either good or evil. Civilizations that once flourished became corrupt. Darkness spread throughout the land, but there were always pockets of light that tried to defeat the evil.

Then Jesus Christ was born on the earth. His message was plain. He said, "Repent, be baptized, and through my sacrifice and teachings let me save you. You are not alone. You are God's children and I am here to remind you of our plan of salvation. I will die for you, and if you repent and keep my commandments, I will pay your debt to justice, so you can live again with our Heavenly Father. I will send the Holy Ghost to comfort, guide and tell you the truth of your earthly existence. All you have to do is live according to my laws and our Father's plan of salvation so you can return home once again."

Jesus Christ defeated Lucifer and took the keys of hell and death from him when Jesus was resurrected from the dead. Thus our Father's plan was triumphant and we could have the hope of returning to our heavenly home and shout for joy once again.

Lucifer said, "You will not win as long as the earth shall stand. I will send my hatred and greed across this land to all mankind. I will pay them with gold and silver and the gems of the world. I will send false priests to confuse them. I will send my armies that obey me to destroy them. I will send a force of my spiritual minions to yell into their minds and confuse and drown out all of your goodness. I will send forth a bloodbath of revenge and blame that will pile your children into early graves."

Jesus said, "Lucifer, you are destined to be defeated and pay for your evilness. God knows all things from the beginning to the end. You will never win the souls of all of God's children. They will choose their Father in Heaven, not you. They will follow me, for I tell them the truth and they will be set free."

Lucifer looked at Jesus and said, "But how many will I destroy before they remember who they really are? I cannot force them, but the allure of my temptations will trap most of them. How many will be left to partake of your plan of salvation? How many?"

50 | THE LIE

This is a story about a little boy that cried wolf. You remember the story from your childhood. He lied so often that no one ever knew if they should believe him. On many occasions when he cried wolf, everyone came running, only to hear his laughter as he deceived them again. He thought it was great fun.

Then one day a disaster really did happen, but when he cried wolf, no one came running at all. The moral of this story is clear: Always tell the truth so others will believe you.

Here is a story that illustrates this point.

The little boy cried wolf as a means of getting attention. He did it so often that it stopped working. So he decided to run away from home. Maybe they would pay attention now.

As he traveled from home, he walked approximately one block and came upon a beggar. He stopped to chat. "Why are you alone and so smelly?"

The beggar looked at him with crooked teeth and the odor of alcohol on his breath and said, "I was a boy like you, and one day I ran away from home. Is that what you are doing? I told lies and stole, and then I ran before they could discipline me and teach me their ways. So I have been wandering around for years. I have gotten used to my sad life now. I don't expect much, but I don't give back anything in return either. Best you go back home, boy, before it's too late."

The boy was quiet but decided to walk on a bit further. In the next block, he came across a little girl playing with her dolls.

"Hi," he said. "I am running away from home, what are you doing?"

She looked at him and said, "I am having a tea party for my dolls. I am serving herb tea and crumpets. Would you like to join us?"

So he did. He drank wonderful-tasting tea in tiny cups and ate crumpets that were really chocolate chip cookies.

The boy said, "This is wonderful, but I got in trouble for pretending, and here you are happy as a lark pretending with your dolls.

The little girl looked at him and replied. "I am not pretending. That is real tea and cookies that you just ate. Everything here is real, and with you here, I really have a party. When I pretend I know that I am truly pretending and I don't call it anything else. Why is this important to you?"

The little boy got up and thanked her for the lovely party and left. He certainly didn't feel any better about running away from home.

In the next block, he came across a family of six. They were barbequing chicken and having a picnic. Boy, that food smelled good. He looked at them with hunger in his belly. The man of the family noticed him and said, "Come eat with us if you are hungry. We have plenty to share." So he did.

He heard them laugh and he saw them interact with their kids. One scraped his knee and they put a bandage on it. Another said the food was too hot so they blew on it to cool it down. Another kid got mad at his friend and sulked in the corner sucking his thumb. Another child said there was someone hurt over the hill and needed help. The father got up and ran to where he pointed. When the father was not looking, the son took his chicken and ate it all.

When the father returned and saw his child laughing, he was not happy. He took that child and spanked him. "Do not lie or steal," he told him. "Once you get into that lying habit, you will be doomed for life. There are consequences to your actions."

The little boy watched all of this with amazement. He saw all this through new eyes and finally understood why everyone was angry with him. He thanked the father for the food and his guidance. He told him how he learned a great lesson in the few short hours he spent with his family.

The little boy turned around and ran back to his home. He ran past the little girl, past the beggar and into the hallway of his house. He flung his arms around his mother's knees and begged for forgiveness. She said, "Son, did you truly learn a lesson? Will you agree never to lie again?"

The little boy said, "Yes, oh yes! I will not do it again." Then she said, "I forgive you my son."

When we lie, steal, or cheat, we can make amends to those we hurt, choose to repent, learn from our mistakes, change, and improve, We can also ask the Lord to forgive us of our sins as well.

51 | THE TRUTH

There was a true spirit of the Lord known as the Holy Ghost. He went around on the earth seeking someone who was truthful. He listened in on conversations. This is what he heard:

The first person thought to himself, "I murdered someone. I will get a great attorney and won't allow myself to go on the stand. Maybe I can get off." But what about the truth? Did he murder that person?

The spirit kept on going, seeking the truthful.

The true spirit visited a business and overheard a conversation with an employee.

"It's not my fault," the employee said. "I didn't have the right information."

"Well," said the employer, "couldn't you have found out the information and taken care of the customer?"

The employee replied, "That is not in my job description. I'm not paid enough to worry about those problems."

"Isn't it your job to take care of the customers?"

"Yes, but it's not my fault."

Actually, the truth was that the employee left his job to meet a friend and he couldn't be bothered with worrying about the customer.

The true spirit was saddened. What a mess. That company was in trouble. No wonder.

The true spirit continued on his quest until he found a highschool yard where he overheard some teenagers talking. But what did the true spirit hear?

"Man, we need to kill that dude. He had the guts to wear our colors and he didn't give me his money when I asked for it. Let's just go shoot him and put a few rounds into his house."

The other boy said, "No, that is not a good idea. You will be caught and have to go to prison."

"Nah, you can tell the police I was here with you."

The true spirit kept searching for people who did not lie, cheat or steal, who did not murder or envy, who did not color the truth and embellish it, who did what was right, or at least tried to.

The true spirit came across a few who really tried to love one another and do what was right. They loved the Lord and abided by his commandments.

They understood that they could receive forgiveness through Christ after truly repenting of their wrongs, making restitution and changing. At least, these people were trying.

The true spirit understood, as they did not, that all lies are known. Without the truth, the people would suffer the consequences past death, and possibly for eternity.

There was a woman who lived by her wits. She walked the streets and tampered with her salvation. She participated in a numb existence, ready to fling herself over the edge.

She saved most of her money so she could send her daughter to a private school. She did not want her daughter to be destroyed along with her.

What was her name? It was Fortified. Now, that is an unusual name for a woman, but it gave her the stamina and hope to live another moment. The mother felt fortified against adversity no matter how awful her life had become.

One night she was walking the streets looking for a customer and found herself instead. How did this happen?

A young, good-looking man approached her and said, "Hi, want to join me and my companions? We have a limousine over there."

She agreed and stepped into the car. The young man drove to an old mansion up on a hill. When she departed from the car, she walked into the house. It was poorly lit and the walls seemed to ooze out slime. It smelled of rotting things and screams of old.

She walked into the room that was filled with people who were definitely evil. She realized that this was not where she wanted to be and was scared.

They said, "We have been waiting for you for many years. We are glad you are here. You are one of us and we thought we should meet. This will be a night you will remember."

As she stepped into the room, her heart pounded. What was she doing here? These were not her kind of people. These were very scary souls. She tried to look into their faces, but she could not see their eyes. All she could see were empty sockets within the skulls of their lives.

She thought of her daughter, safe in the school. She also knew that without the money she would earn, her daughter would be kicked out. She was the sole support of her daughter's life.

They could read her thoughts and laughed at her.

"Do you think your daughter is safe in that school?" they said. "How stupid you are. She is safe for now inside the walls, but without love and support, where do you think she will end up? She is learning her lessons, but she needs to learn more than that. You are a good example for her, don't you think?"

The woman bowed her head in shame. They laughed again.

"Who do you think you are kidding? You have lived on the edge of existence for years. You chose that life. You had other options, but you refused to listen. You are truly one of us now. So why not join us? We can show you a real good time. You are ignorant of any purpose in your life. We love ignorance for it breeds more ignorance and we get more people that way.

"Come on into the dining room. The table is filled with all kinds of goodies. We know you will want to partake. Join us by choice. You already have for years. We just want you to say it and commit to us."

She walked into the dining room that was filled with all kinds of wonderful things—gold, silver, diamonds and silks. She saw her favorite foods and stacks of money piled up in the corner. She saw drugs of all types—cocaine, heroin, tranquilizers and sleeping pills. She saw items of torture next to feathers and comforters. She saw magazines with nude people, and horror movies and television shows spouting profanities. She saw newspapers and billboard ads promoting evil. She saw crowds of people gathered in the courthouses declaring freedom of speech while taking God out of every aspect of their lives. She saw cities laid to waste and people put into institutions because of drugs and alcohol.

She heard the people in this house pointing and laughing. They said, "This event was great; it wreaked havoc on so many people." She saw plagues. She saw them learning how to put minds asleep that resulted in terrible car accidents. She saw classes given on how to lull humans into complacency and bind them within their own ignorance and walls. She saw killing and torture. She saw so much that she couldn't take it all in. She became increasingly more scared.

They said to her, "You are one of us. You have been for years. Welcome home."

Had she really passed the point of no return or was there still time for her to repent and change? Did she still have a choice or was it too late?

53 | FEAR

There once was a coyote who snarled and bared his teeth. His growl warned those who came near of his intentions. He was hated and despised. He was hunted and was shot at. He consumed and butchered without remorse and without conscience.

He ate to fill his belly and do his job as a killing machine.

No remorse. No fear of others.

He sought and killed the weakest, the innocent, the pure, the ones who were the quietest. The loud ones who kicked and screamed sometimes escaped. The ones who lived had prepared, were aware of his presence and protected themselves.

They were warned by both the coyote's smell, and then the sound of his running feet. The odor was putrid, rancid and of death and dying things, the footfalls soft, yet insistent, the breathing, quick and hot. The jaws tore at the body and at the mind. There was no reasoning, only the will to destroy.

How could they win against such a beast?

How could they endure?

They just did, and we can too.

54 | THE SHADOW

There was a shadow cast upon the earth.

One day, as I was walking, I noticed my shadow. It was grey in color and was spread on to the ground upon which I walked. But then I noticed another shadow. This shadow was dark and talked with a human voice. How deceptive, for he looked normal except for his shadow which was black and seemed to be absorbed into the ground it covered.

As this man and his dark shadow approached, I stopped. I just watched him as he neared. The dark shadow seemed to increase in size and started to cover his face as well. His features were dark. He had a wide grin and deep set eyes.

I said a prayer and asked for protection through my faith in Jesus Christ.

As the man approached I stood still, for there was no place to run. He sauntered up and his grin grew wider than his face and his eyes sank deep within his skull.

Then he suddenly stopped, as if struck by something unknown. He stared at me as his shadow disappeared and all that was left was a single beam of light. The man fainted and then woke up.

"What happened?" he asked, "I was all ready to murder you and now I am helpless before you."

I stood straight in his path and asked him his name.

He said it was Lucifer.

I said, "Well, no wonder you lost your strength. My name is Faith."

55 | THE CHOICE TO SIN

What is the effect of sin?

How does it break down your body?
How does it manifest itself in your thoughts and then your actions?
How do you feel afterwards?
Good? Bad? No feeling at all?
Who are you today and tomorrow?

Will it affect other lives? For how long?
Does your decision have an impact on society?
Can you think beyond your own selfish reasons and see if it will have a long
term effect on your life and others?
If you kill someone, then aren't you hurting both your own family and the
family of those you harm?
If you take what does not belong to you, have you destroyed your own self-
worth?
If you hit or harm another human, is there an eternal debt to be paid?
Do the decisions you make now affect your life afterward?

Can you feel the pain or are you numb?
Whose responsibility is this mess?
Yours?
You are the one who committed the act.
You must pay and take responsibility or maybe you can get away with it?

But think again, for you get to pay beyond your death. There must be payment
made in full in the next world to meet the demands of justice and to the
family and friends and the lives you affected, for you will be judged based on
your acts upon this earth.

Do you want to be remembered with hate or love?
Do you want to destroy or help?

The choice belongs to you.

56 | THE JUMPING JACK

There was a time in Jack's life when he wondered why he left the house that day. Everything seemed to go wrong. First, he could not find the keys to his car and he needed to get gas. He was late for work and for a meeting with his boss. Everyone he talked to was also having a bad day. No one was nice on the phone. Everyone just started with the words, "I have a problem." Not, "Hello." Not, "How are you today." Nothing but, "You need to solve this problem and right now!"

Jack closed his eyes and ran his fingers through his hair. He took a deep breath and thought of his responsibilities. He had a mortgage and a car payment. His wife worked but, even so, it was hard to make ends meet. His kids, whom he loved dearly, always wanted more and more things to make them happy. When was it time for him to be happy? When was it time to enjoy life? His wife was always harried and upset. She had more than she could handle. They yelled at each other and slept fitfully.

He worked away at the stack of papers on his desk. Everyone was so demanding. Why couldn't they be nice for once in their lives? Would it hurt them to be NICE?! If everyone had patience and helped, then he could do a better job. He walked away from his desk to try and clear his head of the clutter. He went into the hallway and stopped to get a drink of water. A nice secretary from the next office was also standing there. She was so pretty. She was slender and always seemed to be in control of her life.

Jack said, "Hi."

The secretary responded and smiled.

He asked her, "Do you want to go to lunch with me?"

"Yes," she said. "That would be great."

That was the biggest mistake of the day. He sought his solutions in another relationship, one he thought was uncomplicated. It was just a nice flirtation to make him feel good. Really, it was much more than that. What happened next was even worse.

You know the story and the pain it caused. No one was helped. Everyone was hurt. He stayed married to his wife, but only after many months of counseling. He finally got back into the routine of his life.

Why didn't it work? he thought. I tried to find a way out of the morass and I jumped into the fire. Where did I go wrong?

57 | DO YOU WANT TO CHANGE?

There was a beautiful town surrounded by mountains. It had sunsets of peach-colored glow and snow on top to reflect the light. The town was clean and the shops filled with all kinds of goods to wear and eat. Everything you could want was available for a price. You could eat and drink and be merry. You could hike in the woods and ride your bikes on the trails. You could ride horses and walk into the forests. You could lose your way until it was time to return. You could work very hard and never look up to see the beauty. You could stand alone on a mountaintop and say, "I am here, I have made it to the top."

Then you could say, the top of what?
What do you mean?

The same mountains and the same sunsets will be there next year and next year.
The earth and the ground for walking will always be in place.

How do you walk upon this earth?
Do you hike or bike?
Do you climb mountains or bury yourself alive in your office?

Do you hike up to the top of the mountain and say you have arrived?
You did it.
You have accomplished your goal.
What of a greater reward?

What if I told you about a mountain that you could climb and even command to move?
Would you believe me?

What if I told you that you could expand your mind beyond your human limitations?
Would you be convinced?

What if I told you that you cannot hide in your office, your home, your car, your phone, your golf course, your piney woods or anywhere?
Would you believe me?

What if I told you that there is a plan to pull you out of these holes and into a new life in the light of God.

Would you want to listen?

What if I told you that your reward after your life here ends depends on what you do now.

Would you change?

What if I told you that there is a plan already in place to allow you to repent of your wrong choices and sinful acts and be cleansed.

Would you want to take the plunge to become clean and pure again in the sight of God?

What if I told you that when you were cleansed and kept all of God's commandments, you could receive a gift beyond anything you could imagine that could help you here and now and beyond your earthly death?

Would you want such a gift?

What if I told you that there is more to you than you can see in the mirror reflecting back at you? Would you want to take a better look and see what is really there?

What if I told you that you have a choice now?

But, what if you wait? What then?

The mountains will still be here tomorrow and the next day,

But humans change and come and go.

Is your life so secure that you can know what could happen beyond this moment?

Shouldn't you consider a new alternative?

At least, shouldn't you think about it?

Would it be that hard to talk about it? Read about it? Change?

What is required?

Why don't you find out?

It might save your life for eternity.

baptized

committed
contaminated
content
controlling

demented
drinker
daring

easy
eager

free
frustrated
feminine
faithful
frugal
greedy
giving

hopeful
helpful
happy
honest

kind

lovable
likable
large
long

masculine
morose
manipulative

prayerful
patient
poor
playful

religious
riotous
ridiculous
rich
risk taker

safe
smoker
smiling
small

tactful
tenacious
trustworthy
terrorist
tough
tenacious
tested
targeted
tortured

violent

wasteful

It is not hard to describe yourself in words. Pick some, any one, or add your own. How do you feel? Define your life in words. Put them down in writing. Re-write your words each day and see how they change as your spiritual growth changes. Use the words that God gave us. They are so powerful. They define our lives and create all the good that we can imagine. Start at the beginning and continue on until you understand first yourself and then re-define and use new terms for the new you.

59 | DESIRE

What do you desire in life?
A wonderful family and friends?
Wealth?
A home paid for?
Money in the bank?
A new car?
A job you enjoy?
A higher paying job?
Good looks?
Spouse?
Youth?
Love?
Passion?
Safety?
Stardom?
Joy?
Freedom?
Children?
Health?

Mix these up in the order of importance and add your own.

What else do you desire?
A relationship with God?
Jesus Christ?
The Holy Ghost?
Life eternal?

How do you obtain these?
Love of God
Repentance
Acceptance of Jesus Christ as your Lord and Savior
Baptism
Humble yourself
Atonement
Receiving the Holy Ghost
Responsibility

Love of God
Love your Neighbor

Now how do you begin?
Love
Read and study
Pray
Listen
Repent
Live within God's Laws
Moral values
Responsibility
Patience
Faith
Miracles
Thanking God
Changing
Kindness
Caring

When do you want to start?
Now?
Tomorrow?
Too late?

Have you helped others or harmed them?
Are you proud of your life because you were kind?
Were you honest in your dealings with others?
Have you accomplished your life's work?
Have you loved God and your Savior Jesus Christ and
    followed their commandments?
Have you repented from sin and made amends?

Why not? When are you going to start?

Do you want to look at your life at the end, whenever that is,
and have these words said to you: "IT'S TOO LATE!"

Think about it before it is too late.

60 | HOW DO YOU FEEL TODAY?

"How do you feel today?" I inquired. "You look sad. Is there any way I can help?"

Her friend said, "Oh, how kind of you to care, and how rare a friend you are. I do not deserve your kindness. I have harmed myself and many others with some awful choices that I made. I feel so much pain inside because I know I am to blame. I shouldn't have gone to that party. I shouldn't have had alcohol. I shouldn't have gone home with a stranger. I should not have been surprised with the results. But now I have to wait for three tests results—one for drugs, one for AIDS and one for pregnancy; all of this guilt because I made some very bad choices.

"I want to blame the people who had the party. I want to blame them for serving liquor. I want to blame the man for taking advantage of me. I want to blame everyone else except myself. But I decided to go. I am the one who drank and slept with a stranger. I listened to the wrong thoughts in my head and acted on them without thinking about the results. Why didn't I listen and avoid such a destructive path? Well, I am sick—not from any illness, but as punishment for my own stupid choices! What should I do? I don't think I can live with the consequences. I would rather die than give birth to a sick baby. I am worthless. I am scum."

I looked at my friend who had great sadness. I knew she went to church on Sunday, but she obviously hadn't been paying attention. Or maybe she was not receiving the right information. She had been on this path of destructive behavior for some time. I wondered if she was ready to change. I sat her down and asked her if she wanted to be forgiven for what she did. Did she truly want to change the path that her life was taking? She said, "Oh yes, but tell me how?"

I told her about Jesus Christ and his plan of redemption through repentance. I told her about baptism and becoming clean in the sight of God. I talked for hours and she listened intently. She started to cry with relief.

She was in awe. "Really?" she said. "I can be forgiven? I can have another chance? Can I begin to live with myself again and not carry this pain with me forever?"

"Of course," I said. "You are beginning to understand Jesus Christ's atonement, but you must repent, change and not do it again."

So my friend began to study the gospel of Jesus Christ. After a few weeks she decided to follow a new course and be baptized. She told me that she had prayed to God before she was baptized. She cried and sought the

Lord for his forgiveness. She truly repented and when she was truthful and humbled herself, then she said she felt a great weight lift off her shoulders. She suddenly felt free. What a great blessing this was so that she could change her life. She was ready for her new life; however, she knew this change in her must be permanent.

The next day, she received a letter from her doctor. She was fine. The blood tests were all negative. That night she prayed to God with great Thanksgiving. She was free from the curse of the future and free of her past behavior. She had repented and changed her behavior. She had done it. She never wanted to feel that pain again. She never wanted to live that way again. She now had a bright future.

8 THOUGHTS

61 | THERE IS A TIME

There is a time in every life when lies and deceit could take a back seat to what is right.

There is a time in every life when frustration and fear could give way to commitment.

There is a time in every life when trauma could take over but we stand firm in faith.

There is a time in every life when love could change our world.

There is a time in every life when hopes come true and peace fills us.

There is a time in every life when we realize we are all humans.

There is a time in every life when we recognize our spirit inside us.

There is a time in every life when we are one with God.

There is a time in every life, and the time is now.

62 | WHAT CAN YOU BUY?

What can money buy?

It can buy clothes and cars,
But can it buy harmony and peace?
It can buy houses and planes,
But can it buy love and affection?
It can buy watches and diamonds,
But can it buy solitude and security?
It can buy alarm systems and cameras,
But can it stop fear and hatred?
It can buy alarm clocks and trumpets,
But can it buy contentment and calm?
It can buy furniture and computers,
But can it buy fulfillment and friends?
It can buy clowns and corporations,
But can it buy joy and kindness?
It can buy food and video centers,
But can it buy faith and hope?

It can buy all kinds of things that will make us happy.
But does it work?

It can buy a seat at the symphony,
But will you enjoy the music?
It can buy a plane to fly you anywhere,
But will you enjoy the trip?
It can buy you a party where everyone drinks and eats their fill,
But are they your friends?
It can buy you clothes and expensive perfume,
But do you smell as sweet as the rose growing in your garden?
It can buy companionship and nursing care,
But is there anyone to sit by your side and ease your pain?
It can buy the things of this world,
But what doesn't it buy?
It can buy you a perfect life!

Are you sure?

63 | THE LABEL

What is a label?

The dictionary defines it as "a card, paper, etc. marked and attached to an object to indicate its contents, owner, destination; a term of generalized classification."

Is a label the small, scratchy item stitched inside of your shirt?
Is it the tag on a pillow that says "Do Not Remove"?
Is it a definition of who you are?
> What work you do?
> How many children you have?
> Whether you are a mother, father or child?
> What religion you are?
> What car you drive?
> How much you are worth?
> Where you live?
> What clothes you wear?

There was a young girl who searched for a label. She wanted to define who she was by a simple statement. Let's see. What could she say? How could she try and describe herself using very few words.

She is pretty. She is honest. She is smart. She is nice. She is sincere. She is a hard worker. She is loving. But, she also has a temper. She is impatient. She is greedy. She is sometimes jealous. She is egotistical. She is demanding. Oh, this is getting harder.

She loves her brothers and sisters. She loves her parents. She loves to cook. She hates to clean house. She does not listen very well. She knows it all. She does not know how to balance a checkbook. She loves to tap dance. She is a brunette. She is plump. She is a mother. She is a wife. She is a sister. She is a dentist. She is a....

This could go on. This is not simple. She is too complex. How can she simply label herself? Well, we need to think about this some more.

What about her belief system? She believes in God. She could be a Christian, Jewish, Methodist, Catholic, Baptist, Presbyterian, a Mormon, Hindu, Buddhist, Muslim, etc. There are so many different labels in religion. Maybe she could just say, "I believe in Jesus Christ." Is that enough? Can she define who she is by her belief or does she need a label? Is a label enough to explain everything that she is?

After considering all the labels she could have, she has finally realized the absolute best label that she could have.

Do you know what it is?

She is a daughter of God. How wonderful.

This is a label that is comprehensive, truthful and expresses her fundamental relationship to her Heavenly Father.

64 | THE DOT

Consider a dot. So simple. Just a dot. A little point on a page. An end to a thought. It allows the beginning of a new era. A stopping place, a pause. Just a dot. So insignificant and yet so profound. Without it, we run on forever. What makes it essential are the continuing thought processes needed to connect one idea to another, eventually forming a solution, a situation, a sensitive issue, a dizzying exclamation, a fundamental truth, a declaration of a future.

What is a dot? A small round mark with no beginning and no end.
A circle of belief. A solution and an unending question.
What is a dot? The center of all things—a continuum, a focus, an enigma, a stigma, an end and perhaps a beginning.
The dot allows the sequence of one idea to another that begins and ends at the beginning. What do I mean? You can see a dot. You write it at the end of a sentence, a paragraph, a page, a number, an exclamation point, a question and then it ends.

Focus on the importance of just a dot. Consider that you are more important than a dot, for you make the mark upon the page. You produce the ideas and words that fit together to form the thought. You link the thoughts together and form a conclusion. You create with your dots. You form pictures and ask questions. You exclaim your views. You form the dots into regimens and habits and rituals as you punctuate your lives with ongoing dots and ongoing words.

STOP!

You are more than a dot. You are the maker of the dot. You are the creator and the writer. You are the connector and the center of focus. You are in control of which dot to use and which circle to become. You are in the center of creativity.

What is a dot?
Everything you can imagine and all the responsibility that it entails. Begin with the simplest idea, see how complex it is, and then simplify it again. Unravel the unexplained and accept that some things are true. You were taught to use a dot, a circle and what they are for. You use them in grammar, in symbols, in circles, in life, in patterns to lead forward.

How much more complex can God be than a simple dot. Don't be led down the wrong road of discovery. Look at the simple dot and know your own limitations of creative power. Look to God and know your true value. Learn the lesson of the dot and grow from there. Begin with the dot and go into the circle of life that is God's.

65 | THE STAR OF GOD

There was a star
Beautiful and shining clear in the line of sight,
Lighting the path of planets and lighting the stage of existence of new worlds.

There was a star
Famous in all her beauty,
Wondrous in her charms and powers,
Dynamic and talented.

There was a star
Brighter than the eyes could see,
More distant than the touch of life,
More complex in structure,
More brilliant in illumination.

There was a star
So far away yet so close,
So distant yet unique,
So wondrous yet plain,
So simple.

Just a star
A brightness focused upon the face of the earth,
An enchanting dance,
A noble quest.
So simple.

There is a star
A strong belief,
A hero,
A nurturer,
A lover,
A healer.

GOD

66 | THE WORD

A Word

It can be a profound statement of fact, truth or logic.

It can be a verb, an adjective, a noun, a pronoun.

It can be an amoeba, a protozoa, a plant, an animal, a human.

It can subtract, add, multiply, compute and continue to infinity.

It can thrive, love, enjoy, laugh, dream, hope and endear.

It can work, strengthen, lengthen, solve, formulate, postulate, organize, extend and create.

It can budge, nudge, push, pull, form, inform, judge, indulge.

It can learn, earn, propose, suppose, tantalize and excite.

It can think, believe, perceive, envision, accept and find.

It can understand, learn, return and find the answers to all the riddles, puzzles, misunderstandings and truths.

It is everything and anything.

But who started with the Word?
God!

(According to the Apostle John, the "Word" is the Messiah, Jesus Christ. John 1:1-5)

67 | ENDLESS CLOUDS

The clouds line up across the vastness of the sky as the sun moves through the edges of time. The light flows onward and onward across mountains and lakes, vast fields and ice floes. The white divides in crevices and shifts from plane to plane. Pockets of blue pierce the whiteness as I look beyond the horizon.

What if I lived on the clouds and could never again feel the earth beneath my feet? What if I drifted along in this window of imagination forever? What type of desires could I have as I live in such a cocoon of life? Why would this be appealing? I feel nothing now but calm and peace. I do not have to run anywhere or meet anyone. No decisions need to be made or care given for another. I am not challenged or edified. I do not fear or hate. I have no jealousy or need for money. I am safe as I drift along and fly over the earth.

The constant drone of the airplane's engines is the only reminder that this thought can end.

I am tired and I need to rest, but the sight of the clouds lures me back. What is it like to drift over the clouds of time endlessly? What is it like to savor the quiet calm of the moment? How do I feel when I am not needed every minute of the day? I sit here and reflect on the beauty I see and all else fades, all concerns, all cares and all questions. I just enjoy the view of billowing clouds.

But, I also see the magnificence of the world. I feel the flow of life as it passes by below me. There are so many people moving, pushing, pulling, loving and hating; so much chaos, with pockets of peace here and there. There is not enough time below. But up here, there is all the leisure time in the universe.

What if I found the pocket of time and stepped in for a moment? What if I could stand alone and be part of it all? Would I be alone or part of a vast knowledge of God, the creator of all clouds? Can this be accomplished in this lifetime?

Let me try to retain this sense of balance as I depart along the ground, walking and entering into the playing field of doubt. Let me retain the gifts of my calm and loving spirit against the loud mouths of fear. Let me forsake the calamities of life as I focus on the eternity of truths. Let me be at peace, just as I am now, looking out on the endless procession of white, fluffy clouds that is just outside my view.

68 | THE FOUNDATION

The road to existence lies upon the foundation of God.
The road can be bumpy, rough, smooth, pot-holed or cracked.
It can be straight, crooked, curved or hilly.
It can be wet, cold, hard, soft or tarred.
It can be strewn with debris.
It can be marred and torn or beautiful and perfect.

Each road is the direction in which you walk.
Each corner, the choice by your own will.
Each moment can hold you onto the ground or chase you away with years of
  waste.

How can you exist without a Foundation?
Do you drift along in a fog that filters life through either rose-colored or
  opaque glasses?
Can you see beyond your own state of life?

What is the Foundation upon which you rest?
Is it soft or hard?
Is it strict or lazy?
Is it complacent?
Is it fearful or unnerving?
Is it torn or is it complete?
Is it loving or do you run down the lanes of hatred and greed?
Is it fulfilling or is it disquieting?
Is it happy or is there a yearning for something else?

What is the Foundation of your life?
Is it your family, your friends, your business, your career, your clothing?
Is it your mannerisms, your caring, your friendliness, your warmth, your joy?
Is it your ego, your hatred, your betrayal, your forgetfulness?
Is it your habits, your doubts, your dreams?
Is it your GOD?

What is your Foundation? What should it be?

9 THE END TIMES

69 | THE HERMIT

There lived a hermit in a cave covered with moss and peat. He looked out of the dark hole and only ventured out at night. He stole food and clothes and smelled of long-ago-rotting things. He busied himself plotting hate and tried to lure others to his way of thinking. He was not happy with the world; not at all. They had stolen what was his and he would get it back someday. Every once in a while others came by to listen, for they were unhappy, too. They lost their jobs or they took some drugs. So what? The rich had so much and they had nothing. They deserved a break.

The hermit smiled with yellow teeth and his eyes aglow. "Are there many others like you in the world?"

"Yes, of course."

"Then let's gather them together."

Pretty soon many came complaining of one thing or another, blaming society and the rich, blaming the Jews. They blamed the government. They blamed and blamed everyone and everything except themselves. They needed money so they stole. They needed a place to live so they killed the occupants and took over. They spent their days and nights plotting and planning. Kill and steal. Make them pay. They took over a town and then another. Their rallying cry was, "This belongs to us, not to you," and "We will cleanse the land of all who do not believe as we do." They burned and killed. They did not hear the cries of mothers and children, of fathers whose families were lost and dead. They were consumed with hate. Other groups gave them money and ammunition—arms to continue their war. They kept on and on.

Then one day they stopped, for they had reached the end of the world.

They all turned around and saw only ruins—bombed out shells and crying souls, destitute and hungry people wandering around lost.

Suddenly they realized that they had nothing to replace the world they destroyed. No one was left to care for them. There was no more food, no more ammunition, no more lands or people to destroy. Now what should they do? Their sole purpose and sole energy was hate and revenge. How would they ever rebuild the world? What would they put in its place? They looked to the hermit for the answers.

But he had disappeared and only his laughter was heard.

70 | THE WINDOW

I was sitting next to the window during my flight to somewhere. I watched the evening sky turn from light to dark as the clouds raced by. I looked down upon the earth and saw a city lit up from its core and spread out beyond its borders. Then I saw dots of lights that must have been homes and families fixing their evening meal. I was transfixed as I looked out the window, knowing that we were separated by space, but only that. We have much in common, those people below and the ones here with me. We are each a child of God.

Suddenly, I saw an explosion below. The earth seemed to convulse and fire shot upward into the sky. What was happening? I was trapped in my seat and could not reach them to help. All I could do was look through the window and observe the events as they occurred. I saw the flames pour out upon the earth and consume all that came in their path.

As I looked as far forward as I could, the setting sun glowed with a bright yellow light and reflected the massive changes I saw in the contours of the earth. Again and again I saw the land roll out like dough being kneaded. It was rolled out and smoothed. It was convulsed and cried and groaned as it was forced to change. I saw as it traveled from city to city and blackness enveloped the earth.

The people below could not be seen from my window, for I was too high in the air. I started to pray. I prayed for their safety. I prayed for their survival. I prayed to my Lord to help them.

I prayed for so many things that God said, "I know, little one, but this is the time of change. This is the time of the latter days. This is the time when great faith will be needed by all the children of God. There is only one path to safety and that is through me."

"I know, my Heavenly Father," I replied. "I pray for all of us now for we face great trials and greater change."

Our plane was descending to its destination. I securely fastened my seat belt and braced myself for the landing to come. I prayed again for our safe arrival. Then we landed and I looked out the window again. What I saw brought tears to my eyes. There were thousands of people lining the runway, all on their knees praying to Heavenly Father through their Savior and Redeemer. The light was not from electricity, nor the moon. The light was from Jesus Christ and no other source could be seen by the human eye.

It had begun.

Were we ready?

71 | THE BADGE

The elegant woman rose from the leather cushions in her limousine and stood before a large building. She wore an emerald-studded shawl and a dress of the finest silk. Her hair was piled high on her head. Her demeanor was regal and her voice quiet but strong. She knew who she was.

She walked with assurance and pride. She commanded attention and controlled events around her. She was arrogant as she looked sharply at those near her and dictated instructions. Her voice was harsher now and more demanding. "You know who I am so obey my words."

The people cringed and hung their heads. "Yes, ma'am," they said. "Yes, of course. Right away."

She wore a badge made of diamonds, sapphires and precious gems of this world. Her eyes were hooded and surrounded with dark lines. Her lips were bright red and her laugh loud and high in volume. She demanded attention right now!

"Lest you forget" she stated, "I have this badge so do not disobey me."

She walked further on into the building and her hand caught the sleeve of a young man. "Who are you? What is your name?" she demanded.

He looked up from his work and stared into the black-lined eyes and smiled.

"How dare you smile when you look at me?" she said. "Don't you know who I am?"

He smiled again and she shuddered.

"Of course I know who you are," he replied. "I see your badge, but I also know how you received such a mark upon you."

She was angry at his insolence. She lashed at his face with her fingernails and left a red streak across his cheek.

He did not flinch. He simply looked at her with great warmth and love. She shrieked at him and grabbed his shoulders. She turned him around and shoved him into the crowd.

"You have no right to look at me that way!" she yelled. "Depart from my sight. You don't have a badge and I do!"

The young man had fallen to his knees when she shoved him. He knelt in prayer and asked his heavenly Father, through Jesus Christ, to guide and protect him and his place on this earth. As he prayed and asked for God's light and love to crush the darkness, he heard a scream of torment.

She yelled, "I have a badge! You have no right!"

He prayed and prayed and soon those around him joined him on their knees. The woman's eyes glowed redder and her appearance changed in front of them.

Everyone called upon the Lord to save them.

Then all was quiet. No more screams were heard. The people opened their eyes and looked around.

All that was left of the woman was a pile of clothes and other things. On the top was the badge, but instead of diamonds the badge was only tin. It was rough edged and worn down. It was just a piece of worthless metal, nothing of value at all.

The young man of faith picked up the piece of tin and cupped it in his hand. He went over to the trash can and threw it in. What a worthless piece of trash. Her badge was all show and no substance. It glittered and mesmerized. It commanded attention. But the true badge was the young man's faith in Jesus Christ. He knew that the Lord's mark was upon his heart. It was not for display for everyone's eyes. It was a true badge of courage for it was hidden in the core of his soul.

The people started murmuring; doubt and blame crept into their words. It wasn't our fault she died. It was his. They started pointing fingers and turning their backs. Soon the trash can started to shake. Everyone could hear the tin badge as it hit the sides. Fear coursed through their minds and many ran outside to escape.

The young man just stood there. He was rooted to the spot. He smiled and called after them to be not afraid. He looked with love at them, but most left anyway. Those that stayed surrounded the trash can and commanded silence in the name of Jesus Christ.

It was quiet again, except for the still soft voice of God.

10 YOUR STORY

Write your own story here. Keep it to yourself or share it with your friends. Write your story today and then next year and the next and see what changes you have made.

www.ingramcontent.com/pod-product-compliance
Lightning Source LLC
Chambersburg PA
CBHW071003040426
42443CB00007B/646